True Crime— The '70s

13 Shocking True Crime Cases from the 1970s

Alexander Dragone

consult a licensed professional before attempting any techniques outlined in this book.

By reading this document, the reader agrees that under no circumstances is the author responsible for any losses, direct or indirect, that are incurred as a result of the use of the information contained within this document, including, but not limited to, errors, omissions, or inaccuracies.

Contents

1

Introduction

You are about to start a journey into the dark underbelly of the 1970s, where real-life horrors unfolded in chilling detail across continents. Brace yourself for a journey through the minds of some of the most notorious criminals in history. This decade bore witness to cultural revolutions and political upheavals, yet it also became an unsettling breeding ground for infamous figures whose crimes shook the world to its core.

The 1970s were a time of change and transformation. The world was shifting in ways that seemed chaotic and unpredictable. Governments faced crises, societies grappled with new values, and technology brought people closer together while also exposing them to unprecedented dangers. But amid these seismic shifts lurked shadows—unseen threats that would later be revealed in haunting detail.

Cut through the noise of disco music, political protests, and revolutionary ideas, and what you will find is a darker narrative intertwined with the rattling chains of crime. It was as if the tumultuousness of the age provided cover for sinister minds to work their evil deeds. Henry Kissinger, Watergate, and Vietnam are some of the defining features of this decade, but so too are Ted Bundy, John Wayne Gacy, and Dennis Rader—names that are now synonymous with terror and tragedy.

Ted Bundy's chilling charisma masked a malignant predator that lurked behind a seemingly benign exterior. His calculated approach to luring victims sent shivers down the collective spine of society. John Wayne Gacy's deceptive mask of normalcy hid monstrous behaviors that would horrify even the most hardened detectives. Meanwhile, Dennis Rader operated in cold detachment, his letters to the police taunting them as he continued his spree unchecked for years. Each of these individuals presented a complex fabric of motivations, behaviors, and psychological peculiarities that continue to fascinate and horrify us today. And they are just some of the names on this infamous list.

All those criminals deployed their deadly rallies in the United States, but this book doesn't stop at the borders. Crime and evil don't recognize geographical frontiers.

Prepare for a global exploration that uncovers the grim tales from Europe, Australia, and Canada, unraveling the interconnected web of darkness that spanned continents. In England, the atrocious murders carried out by the Yorkshire Ripper left an indelible scar on the nation. Even far-off Australia wasn't immune, grappling with its own chilling cases that defied logic and explanation. Sometimes, criminals started their raids in one country and moved to another, evading lawmen for years.

Mass murders didn't just affect isolated families: They tore apart entire communities, staining the social fabric with fear and suspicion. Examining these events allows us to understand the psyche of the perpetrators and the resilience and vulnerabilities of different communities. We aim to learn about true crime to deal with the fear of all the cruelty some human beings are capable of—and also to be comforted by the idea of achieving justice when the killers are finally convicted. Moreover, we need to know that beyond the horror, communities are always ready to fight against evil.

In the United States alone, over 100,000 crimes were committed during the 1970s. It is impossible to cover them all, but this selection provides insights into some of the most resounding. Some of them became infamously popular for the atrocity of the crimes, others for the magnitude of the killing rides, and some others for the level of violence that unfolded against the victims. For any or all of those reasons, the cases gathered in this collection had the power to move people's empathy and catch the media's attention.

Not all horror stories end with capture and justice served. Some cases remain unsolved, lingering in the collective consciousness, haunting us with unanswered questions and unresolved fears. Claire Gagnon's murder became a cold case, and Gary Allan Srery remained in that condition for decades until the truth was brought to light. These mysteries serve as stark reminders of the limitations of forensic science and the enduring enigma of human malevolence.

Sit comfortably and get ready to enter a world where reality is stranger—and more terrifying—than fiction. Welcome to a journey through the darkest corridors of the 1970s.

Bind, Torture, Kill

Dennis Rader, infamously known as BTK, terrorized Kansas from 1974 to 1991. Most serial killers have tormented early lives and struggled for years with their criminal ideations, developing their killer instincts little by little. Unlike others who start with assaults and minor crimes, Rader started with a big and outrageous attack on a whole family.

Joseph Otero was 38 years old and had an ordinary life with his wife, Julie, and their children. Josephine and Joseph Jr., 11 and 9 years old, respectively, were the youngest and were at home on the fatal night Rader broke into their house.

Early in the morning on January 15, 1974, BTK waited outside the Oteros residence, where he had lurked for a while. He had chosen them as his victims, though the original plan wasn't to murder them but only to rob them. He sought money and the car, but things turned out differently.

Rader had gone through the plan time after time: He would enter the house, confront Julie with a pistol, and threaten the younger children. Then, he would take the car, the money, and everything of value before leaving. Nonetheless, he hadn't considered that Joseph, the father, might also be home. Joseph's presence made Rader go out of his mind and lose control. Once he started killing, he couldn't stop.

The first step was to enter the house without raising suspicions. At 7:30 p.m., Joseph opened the back door to let the dog out. It was the moment Rader was waiting for. Once inside the house, he cut the telephone lines and walked into the dining room, where four members of the family were gathered. The older children weren't at home.

Pointing at them with a pistol, Rader ordered the family to lie on the floor, but then, he thought he was too exposed as the front windows were open. He ordered the family to go to the bedroom. Mr. and Mrs. Otero begged him to let the children go away while promising to give him anything he wanted. But their pleas and tears didn't move the killer.

As they entered the bedroom, BTK ordered the Oteros to lie on the floor again, still at gunpoint. This time, the killer tied them up. He would later say he wanted Joseph to be comfortable and even helped him place a pillow under his head while he was tied to the floor. In his twisted mind, Rader thought he was being kind to the family he was torturing.

The Oteros continued begging him to release them. The children cried because the ropes around their wrists hurt them. Julie tried to keep the children calm and advised them not to yell. She believed that if they collaborated with him, he would just leave without harming them. Joseph offered Rader his car, money, and watch, and he promised not to call the police.

Rader thought about leaving, but then he realized he had skipped some significant details in his plan. Until that moment, Rader hadn't thought of the consequences of his attack. He realized he wasn't wearing a mask or anything, and the victims had seen his face. There was only one thing he could do.

Rader went to the kitchen and grabbed a plastic bag. He came back to the bedroom and put it over Joseph's head while his family was watching. He pulled a rope around his neck to fasten the bag and left him to suffocate. He stopped when he thought Mr. Otero was dead. Then, Rader walked toward Mrs. Otero and put his hands around her neck. He strangled her. She fainted, and Rader thought she was dead, too.

Then, he went for the children and did the same. Joseph Jr. made a hole in the bag, and when Rader realized, he used a T-shirt to cover his head and put another bag over the cloth. Then, he took the boy to another bedroom. The little girl was already dead on the bed.

Mrs. Otero woke up to find the tragedy that had happened to her family, and Rader came back to strangle her again. This time, he used a cord, and this time, he didn't stop until making sure she wasn't breathing anymore. Rader didn't want to leave any witnesses, so he strangled the father again in case he wasn't dead yet.

This brutal murder marked the beginning of a pattern. He would often break into homes, bind his victims using ropes or other restraints, torture them mentally and physically, and then finally kill them. The meticulous nature of his crimes was alarming. He took trophies from his victims, such as clothing or personal items, which he used later to relive the murders through fantasy.

In October of the same year he killed the Oteros, Rader left a letter to the authorities at the Wichita Public Library. He described, in chilling detail, what he had done to the couple and their children. He was proud of what he did and even told the police what they should call him. He wrote, "The code words for me will be... Bind them, Torture them, Kill them, B.T.K."

He adopted the acronym BTK to label his crimes, branding himself for infamy. That revealed another side of his personality: his narcissism. In one letter to authorities, he wrote, "How many do I have to kill before I get a name in the paper or some national recognition?" This statement epitomizes his desire for notoriety. He saw himself as a natural predator, akin to a venomous snake, dismissing any responsibility for his actions by attributing them to an internal force he called "Factor X." This self-perceived compulsion to kill removed any sense of guilt or remorse.

Rader displayed traits typical of psychopathy: manipulative behavior, lack of empathy, and grandiosity. Despite his heinous acts, he managed to lead a seemingly normal life. He was a Boy Scout leader and a compliant family man, which made him even more dangerous as he hid in plain sight. His ability to switch between his two personas—devoted community member and sadistic killer—showcases his fractured psyche.

The evolution of Rader's behavior over time shows a clear progression. His early crimes were highly organized, reflecting detailed planning and control. As years passed, his killings became less frequent but no less brutal. The significant gap between his last two murders (13 years) was unusual compared to other serial killers. During this period, he satisfied his urges through elaborate fantasies and autoerotic activities. He claimed these fantasies prevented him from killing more frequently, believing society owed him gratitude for showing restraint.

Rader perpetrated his last proven crime in 1991. On January 19, he threw a brick through a window to access the house of his chosen victim. He seemed to have a less sophisticated plan or to be less cautious than at the beginning. This time, the victim was a 62-year-old woman named Dolores Davis. She was alone, and BTK had no issues to overpower her. He strangled Dolores with a pair of pantyhose he found in her bedroom. Then, he put a mask on Dolores's face and put her in his car. Rader drove and hid the body under a bridge.

BTK's reign of terror left deep scars on the Wichita community. The psychological aftermath for residents was profound and long-lasting. Living under the constant threat of an unknown, elusive killer created a pervasive sense of fear and anxiety. For many, everyday tasks became laced with dread; even mundane activities felt dangerous. People double-checked locks, avoided going out alone at night, and developed hyper-vigilant behaviors. Families were particularly affected, as parents struggled to protect their children from the lurking menace while coping with their own fears. This era marked a period where safety, once taken for granted, became a luxury many no longer felt they could afford. They didn't feel safe, and actually, they weren't.

The police were unsuccessful in explaining who the killer of Wichita was, and for many years, he walked freely through the streets. He could be anywhere, spying on families and picking the next victim, just waiting for the best moment to strike. He had proven his timing was unique, and so were his motivations: He wanted attention and recognition.

The media played a significant role in shaping public perception of Rader's crimes. Sensationalized coverage often prioritized shocking headlines over sensitive reporting. Newspapers and television broadcasts frequently highlighted gruesome details and lurid aspects of the BTK case, which, while capturing public attention, also served to heighten community fear. This approach led many residents to feel that they were living in a horror movie, as each new report seemed to amplify the danger and unpredictability of BTK's actions. Moreover, the extensive media coverage may have inadvertently fueled Rader's ego, giving him the notoriety he craved. As his communications with the media showed, he relished the attention, using it as a stage to taunt law enforcement and the public alike.

For many years, there was no trace of BTK, and the name "Denis Rader" wasn't even mentioned. One day, in

2004, a local newspaper, The Wichita Eagle, published a note to commemorate the anniversary of the Oteros massacre. That ignited BTK's anxiety about being in the headlines again and led him to reestablish his twisted correspondence with the authorities. It was the beginning of a cat-and-mouse play between the criminal and the police that would eventually lead to solving the cases of at least 10 crimes in the city between 1974 and 1991.

The letters to the police were part of his *modus operandi* and his strategy to spread fear as much as his killing rituals and victim profiles. It took over a year to unravel the mystery and discover who was behind the atrocious acronym chosen by the killer himself.

Some days after the note about the Oteros, The Wichita Eagle editors received a disturbing envelope. Inside, they found a copy of Vicki Wegerle's driving license and photographs of her body. She had been found strangled in her own bedroom in 1986. Her husband entered the room and found Vicki lying on the floor with her hands and feet tied—she had been strangled. Rader had disguised as a phone repairman, and Vicki let him in. Once inside, he pointed her with a pistol and choked her with a nylon stocking. He abandoned the house without being seen. Vicki's husband was blamed for the crime at the time. Now, the police had a clue that Vicki's murder was another one on BTK's record.

The envelope with Vicki's license and photos was the first message. Then, Rader sent a letter with a puzzle to KAKE-TV. Once the specialists could solve the riddle, they discovered the message hid the name "Rader" and an address. Why was Rader leading the cops to him?

And that wasn't all. For months, BTK left boxes and packages in public places. In January 2005, the killer left a garbage bag with another victim's license and a Barbie doll with a hood on the head and the hands tied at her back.

The packages with horrifying clues of the murders continued. The police decided to make a risky move and used a covered agent to attract Rader. They started exchanging messages through newspaper advertisements. One day, Rader sent the policeman a computer disk with data. Yet, the interesting clue wasn't inside the disk. A hacker found out the disk had been used by a man named "Dennis" at "Christ Lutheran Church" and "Park City Library." They crossed the name and addresses and came up with the killer's identity: Dennis Rader, a Christ Lutheran Church's president.

He was arrested on February 25, 2005. A nightmare that began in the 1970s finally came to an end. After confronting DNA evidence against him, BTK confessed he had tortured and killed 10 people. Since he committed the crimes before Kansas re-established capital punishment, Rader was sentenced to 10 consecutive life terms in prison. Even though he will never be released from prison, the horror he unfolded didn't disappear. In 2023, justice discovered new victims linked to BTK.

How many people did he truly kill?

3

The Charming Mr. Bundy

This is the story of a man with a troubled childhood and a captivating yet sinister persona who became one of the most feared serial killers in American history. Ted Bundy was a seemingly ordinary individual who transformed into a calculating murderer.

His first known crime took place in Seattle. The victim was Lynda Ann Healy, a student in the University District. In 1974, she was 21 years old and had entered her senior year of college. She was full of life and lived with four other girls near the university campus. Nothing in her life could have anticipated the monster she was going to meet.

Every morning, Lynda woke up at 5:30 a.m. to go to work. She was the weather girl in Northwest Ski Reports at a local radio station. Nonetheless, that morning of February 1, Lynda didn't show up at the station. It was unusual because she had never missed a day at her job. However, her workmates didn't worry; young students used to hang out and party, so perhaps she hadn't heard her alarm clock.

Lynda had been at a bar the previous night, but that wasn't the reason why she didn't go to work. She hadn't fallen asleep. Her roommate, Barbara, found her bed empty early that morning. Barbara heard Lynda's alarm from her room and thought it was weird that she wouldn't stop it. She was astonished to find out Lynda wasn't in her bed. The bed was undone, so she must have been there earlier, but the room was empty. There was no sign of stress or fight except for a few drops of blood on the pillow and sheets. Was it possible that Lynda had been attacked and Barbara, in the next bedroom, didn't hear a sound?

The room was completely neat, but there was one concerning finding: Inside the wardrobe, the police found Lynda's nightgown covered in blood around the neck. They were certain that Lynda had been attacked and abducted, though they couldn't know if she was still alive. The bloody garment suggested that the aggressor had dressed her up before taking her and took the time to clean the place—everything without making noise and leaving no trace behind.

Her body would remain missing for a long time until it was discovered in 1975 with several others on Taylor

Mountain. There, Ted Bundy had a sanctuary with the bodies of the women he abducted and killed. Lynda had been strangled. This crime set a chillingly similar pattern: young women disappeared without a trace, only for their remains to be discovered later, sometimes never at all. Nobody could guess that young girls who attended college, between 18 and 25 years old, with long hair parted in the middle, were at the sight of a psycho. Girls with similar routines and hobbies had no way of knowing that while they were confidently walking around parks, campuses, and shopping malls, a predator with a thirst for blood was behind their steps.

Between April 1974 and October 1975, following almost a monthly schedule, Bundy kidnapped and killed students. During the next three years, he didn't stop, although the crimes became less frequent—at least those discovered by the police or confessed by him during the trial.

Donna Gail Manson (19), Susan Elaine Rancourt (18), Roberta "Kathy" Parks (20), Brenda Carol Ball (22), and Georgeann Hawkins (18) were kidnapped on their university campuses in Washington state. Until then, there were no clues that led to any suspect. Nonetheless, in July 1974, the police got the first hint that would later unravel Bundy's method.

On a beautiful summer day, Janice Anne Ott (23) and Denise Naslund (19) were enjoying a picnic at Lake Sammamish. They disappeared while surrounded by many people and were never seen again. Nonetheless, some witnesses said they had been talking to a man called "Ted." Bundy was becoming more confident and abducting two women instead of one, but he made a mistake this time.

Even with the police looking for a man named Ted, Bundy didn't stop. On the contrary, he spread his scope, moving to Utah. As part of his ritual, Bundy continued to take his victims to Taylor Mountain, although many of them were reported missing but never found again. Those victims whose bodies weren't at the mountain weren't recovered, and the cases were only solved after Bundy admitted to killing them.

Even though Bundy followed a strict *modus operandi* to kidnap his victims, it was almost impossible for the police to connect the crimes. Victims disappeared in different states. In 1975, Bundy went to Colorado to continue with his deadly hunting, though more crimes were reported in Utah as well. This added confusion to the investigators. Additionally, Bundy extended the age range of his victims: This time, he chose younger victims.

Bundy had a dual personality, marked by charm and brutality that framed dozens of cruel attacks on young women in several states of the U.S. What contributed to developing his darkest side? After his capture, psychiatrists and specialists analyzed him and believed that Bundy's violent behavior, such as his troubled family dynamics and significant childhood trauma, drove him toward his gruesome acts. Bundy's upbringing and psychological factors played a crucial role in shaping his criminal behavior.

Bundy's early childhood was marked by significant trauma. He was born to a single mother, Louise Cowell, at a time when illegitimacy carried a social stigma. To avoid the shame, Bundy was told that his grandparents were his parents and that Louise was his older sister. He would later confess that he always suspected his sister was actually his mother, and this deception undoubtedly contributed to identity confusion and trust issues. His relationship with his mother was complex. Though she provided for him and ensured his physical needs were met, her attention was divided among Bundy and his four half-siblings. This division likely fostered feelings of neglect in Bundy, who later expressed a sense of being unloved despite acknowledging his mother's efforts.

Adding to the turmoil, the tension between Bundy and his stepfather, Johnnie Bundy, who was his real grandfather, often provoked conflict. Ted's materialistic desires clashed with Johnnie's working-class means, leading to friction and a lack of mutual respect. There were accounts of his grandfather being abusive, both physically and psychologically, toward family members, including Bundy. These early experiences of abuse and deception may have fueled Bundy's disdain for authority figures and contributed to his rebellious and deceptive behavior.

As a child, Bundy exhibited troubling behaviors that hinted at a propensity for violence. Once, Bundy was at a Boy Scout camp and, for no reason, took a stick and hit one of his fellow scouts on his head. He also dug holes in the ground and covered them with vegetation to trap unsuspecting victims, reflecting a fascination with causing harm. Such behaviors, coupled with accounts of animal cruelty, where Bundy reportedly pulled apart mice, showed an early inclination toward exerting control over others' lives.

According to psychological studies conducted on him after he was captured, he was a psychopath. Psychopathy is defined by traits such as charm, manipulation, callousness, and a lack of remorse. Bundy exemplified many of these characteristics, even in the early years when he chose to cause harm to amuse himself. He was known to be charismatic and articulate, which allowed him to lead a double life and evade suspicion for many years. This duality allowed him to appear normal while harboring violent tendencies, which made him particularly dangerous.

As he got older, he developed a personality that blended antagonistic traits like deceptiveness, manipulation, and arrogance. He also exhibited high extraversion, as he was engaging and assertive, and high conscientiousness, being organized and diligent. Interestingly, Bundy had low neuroticism, which gave him fearlessness and superficial charm. This explains why he was able to manipulate people effectively, plan meticulously, and execute his crimes without succumbing to panic or guilt.

During his teenage years, Bundy became involved with the Methodist Youth Fellowship, where he even served as vice president. Despite this seemingly positive engagement, Bundy's darker inclinations persisted. The combination of kind attitudes with violent inner forces was a constant throughout his life. He didn't always seek to harm. For instance, on one occasion, he saved a friend's niece from drowning, indicating an ability to perform heroic acts. Yet, he continued to break laws by shoplifting ski equipment and forging lift tickets. Specialists explain that this didn't mean Bundy was good; instead, he sought approval and admiration. His underlying impulsive and antisocial tendencies dominated his actions.

As he grew up, Bundy was able to disguise those antisocial traits and, at the same time, acquired the abilities he needed to release all the evil he cultivated inside. Despite his tumultuous childhood, Bundy left behind the bullies he suffered and the shyness that made him more of a victim than an aggressor. He grew up and developed a cunning and charming personality—traits that masked his dark intentions. Even though he engaged in many violent episodes during his adolescence, most people didn't notice the evil inside him. He seemed kind and friendly, but it was all part of his macabre plan.

Nobody knows for sure when he started killing. Bundy's first known victim was Lynda, found in 1974, but the terrifying characteristics of the crime revealed an experienced killer. It couldn't have been his first one. It is believed that Bundy started killing when he was a teenager...

It was a warm night in August 1961 when Ann Marie Burr, an eight-year-old girl, mysteriously vanished from her house in Tacoma. That night, Ann Marie's parents and sister were inside the house. The family was sure that the girl wasn't playing outside since it was late, and they were getting ready to have dinner. When the mother called her, she didn't show up. They looked around the house and the neighborhood, calling her by her name and asking everybody, but there were no signs. She disappeared without a trace. All they found was an unlocked front door, an open window, and a footprint in the garden. Nobody heard the girl scream, and there were no signs of violence. It was as if she had known her kidnapper.

Who would dare kidnap a girl from her house while everybody is awake? Did the little girl voluntarily leave with her kidnapper? Where was she taken? These questions were never answered since Ann Marie's body was never found. Nonetheless, the scene of the disappearance had many points that, many years later, made the family and the police believe it could have been Bundy's first crime.

By then, Bundy was only 14 years old and lived a few miles away. He used to deliver the newspaper in the neighborhood and spent some time there while visiting an uncle. That gave him the perfect occasion to spy on the families and pick a victim. Moreover, he might have befriended the little girl.

The police could never prove it was him, and he denied it until the very moment of his execution. Nonetheless, the circumstances of Ann Marie's disappearance were very much alike to many of the abductions he committed during his criminal life.

Bundy chose helpless females who would trust him and even wanted to help him. He developed a method that allowed him to approach his victims without scaring them. If they wanted to resist, it was too late. He abducted most of his victims while other people were nearby as if he enjoyed the risk of being caught. It might have increased the adrenaline and sense of control. It is possible to believe that Bundy had bonded with Ann Marie, leading her to do as he told her that night.

Having other people around and persuading the victim to trust him became part of the *modus operandi* to capture his victims. Then, deception was followed by uncontrollable violence.

Bundy deployed a premeditated deceptive strategy to approach his victims. He used to get out of his car, a Volkswagen Beetle, carrying books. He used fake casts or crutches to appear vulnerable. His hunting area encompassed university campuses and nearby colleges, and most of his victims were students. A charming, good-looking man carrying books who looked like an injured student made him an unpredictable threat to unsuspecting young women.

His last horror raid was in Florida on January 15, 1978. Bundy had just escaped from jail, and as he was on the road avoiding the police, he passed near the Chi Omega sorority house near Florida State University. Bundy parked the stolen car he was driving and entered the house. It was 3:00 a.m., and the students were asleep. The psycho entered a room and brutally beat Margaret Bowman and Lisa Levy before finally strangling them to death. Not satisfied with this, he left the room and entered the next one. There, he took his second pair of victims, Kathy Kleiner and Karen Ann Chandler, though they survived.

The pattern was broken. Bundy was out of his mind, and instead of abducting women to kill them privately, he was compulsively killing as many as he could wherever he found them. He attempted one last attack that morning. After he left the sorority house where he thought he had killed four women, he entered another apartment a few blocks away.

A dance student named Cheryl Thomas was sleeping in her bedroom when Bundy broke in and started beating her. It is unclear why he stopped, but Cheryl miraculously saved her life. She suffered a permanent deafness but lived to tell her story. Her testimonial was decisive in Bundy's final apprehension.

Ted Bundy's criminal history was marked by daring escapes and close calls that added to his infamy. One significant event happened on August 16, 1975, when Bundy was arrested in Granger, Utah, after a police chase. Officers found tools like masks, gloves, rope, and handcuffs in his car. Bundy was released on bail, giving him the chance to continue his crimes.

In another escape in June 1977, Bundy jumped out of a courtroom window in Aspen, Colorado, during a hearing. He managed to stay on the run for eight days before being caught again. His most dramatic escape was on December 30, 1977, when he broke out of jail through a hole in the ceiling and then went on a deadly spree in Florida, leading to the tragic murders at the Chi Omega sorority house in January 1978 when Bundy was finally caught.

After his arrest, Bundy faced legal battles where he acted as his own lawyer. He was found guilty and sentenced to prison but continued to face charges related to other murders. His escapes and demeanor during trials emphasized his manipulative behavior. Bundy fled from custody twice, demonstrating his ability to plan and scheme before being recaptured.

The trials that followed Bundy's final capture were marked by intense media coverage and public fascination. Bundy utilized his charm and intelligence in court, often acting as his own lawyer and cross-examining witnesses. Despite his attempts to sway the jury, Bundy was convicted of the Chi Omega murders and sentenced to death. His defense strategies included questioning the reliability of forensic evidence, such as bite marks found on one of the victims, which he claimed could not be conclusively linked to him. However, these efforts were ultimately in vain, as the overwhelming evidence against him led to multiple convictions and death sentences.

The decision to execute Bundy was met with both support and controversy. For many, the death penalty was seen as a fitting punishment for a man who had taken so many innocent lives. However, others argued that execution was not the solution, suggesting that Bundy should spend the rest of his life in prison, reflecting on his crimes. On January 24, 1989, Ted Bundy was executed in the electric chair at Florida State Prison. His final moments were somber, with Bundy mumbling his last words to his lawyer, Jim Coleman, and the Methodist minister, Fred Lawrence, who had prayed with him throughout the night. Crowds outside the prison cheered, "Burn, Bundy, burn!" as the notorious killer was put to death.

4

The Killer Clown

December 13, 1978, was a cold night and the cold and the darkness seemed a terrifying omen for the small community of Des Plaines, Illinois. The local police knocked on the door of a yellow brick ranch house located at Summerdale Avenue. The owner was a popular figure in town. His name was John Wayne Gacy, and he was a beloved neighbor known for his charming and funny performances as a clown at children's parties.

The police weren't searching for the clown. Instead, they were acting on a search warrant. A young man named Robert Piest was reported missing, and the clues led the police to Gacy's door.

Robert was 15 years old at the time, and his mother came to get him after work at a pharmacy. Instead of going home, Robert told his mother he had to meet a contractor about a better job opportunity. He never came back. Robert's mother waited hours for her son to come home, and after a while, she went to the police. As she described the situation, the police realized that the contractor was Gacy. They opened an investigation and found out he had been convicted in Iowa for sexually abusing a teenager.

Without many details, the police scrutinized Gacy's home. There were no signs of Robert; instead, they found many disturbing items in the house. Gacy had shackles and handcuffs in the attic. When the police asked Gacy about that stuff, he answered that he used them to teach escape tricks to children when he performed as a clown. The police didn't buy that story and kept searching. As they examined the house, they reached the garden. The discovery of human remains in the crawlspace beneath Gacy's home was the first unsettling clue to the full extent of his horrifying crimes.

As they began to dig through the crawlspace, investigators faced unimaginable scenes. The smell of decomposition was overwhelming, and the sight of human bones confirmed their worst fears. Over the next several days, bodies were being exhumed one after another, revealing a chilling graveyard right under Gacy's home. Each shovel of dirt unearthed more remains, signaling a methodical and callous execution of victims who had been stripped of their future.

Robert Piest wasn't there. Instead, it was the grave of dozens of victims. Yet, Robert could be connected to Gacy because of a photograph. Gacy had taken a picture of the young boy, which the police found in the trash. The criminal couldn't explain why he had it. Later, it was known that he monitored his victims. His role within the community gave him the opportunity to approach children and teenagers.

John Wayne Gacy—the Killer Clown—had an outward persona that starkly contrasted with his gruesome crimes. His family and neighbors saw him as a generous and engaged member of society. He was married twice, hosted neighborhood parties, and even performed as a clown at children's events. His role as Pogo the Clown endeared him to many, and he was often seen entertaining children and adults alike. This warm and sociable image concealed his dark inner life, where he viewed his victims as mere objects, devoid of humanity.

Professionally, Gacy was successful. He ran his own construction business, PDM Contractors, Inc., providing jobs and seemingly contributing positively to the local economy. He was also a Democratic precinct captain and involved in several civic organizations. Despite these roles, there were warning signs that went unnoticed or were ignored. For instance, Gacy's frequent interactions with young men, who he hired for short-term work projects, raised no suspicions among those who knew him professionally. It is a sobering thought that someone who performed so many public good deeds could harbor such malevolent intentions.

Several factors contributed to Gacy's criminal behavior, rooted deeply in psychological issues. His childhood was marred by a physically and verbally abusive father, which likely instilled feelings of inadequacy and anger. These early experiences may have shaped Gacy's view of the world and influenced his later actions. Psychiatrists said he projected his hatred onto his victims, leading to his uncontrollable compulsion to kill. This psychological portrait painted Gacy not only as a cold-blooded killer but as a deeply disturbed individual wrestling with internal demons.

The identification of victims like William Bundy, a construction worker, and Jimmy Haakenson, who phoned his mother from Chicago before disappearing, wasn't straightforward either. Bundy's remains were identified using dental records in 2011, and Haakenson's identification came in 2017 through DNA analysis, showing the painstaking efforts required to close these tragic cases.

Before becoming a serial killer, Gacy had incurred several offenses of physical abuse to boys and young men. However, one night, he would cross a line that would unleash an even more brutal side of his personality.

Timothy McCoy was a blonde, kind, and funny 16-year-old teenager. His friends called him Tim and said wherever he went, he turned into the "life of the party." On January 2, 1972, Tim said goodbye to his family and left home. Later, he headed to the Greyhound bus station in Chicago and boarded a bus to go back home to Nebraska. However, he would never make it home.

While he was waiting for the bus, a car stopped. The man inside offered him a ride and persuaded him to enter the car. The man drove to his house and invited the boy in. Before Tim could react, the man, who was nobody other than the killer clown, jumped on him and stabbed Tim in his chest.

Tim's family didn't know the truth of what happened until 14 years later when the police found a blood stain under Gacy's bed. Gacy first told his own version of the story: Tim had agreed to join him and stay for the night instead of traveling home for hours. He woke up in the middle of the night and found the teenager walking toward him with a kitchen knife in his hand. They fought, and Tim fell over the knife. It was all a lie. The killer clown confessed later that night he discovered the thrill he experienced by torturing and taking somebody's life.

This was the first time Gacy killed, and it was the only murder when he stabbed the victim. For his other victims, he used his own hands to strangle them. Gacy perpetrated most of his crimes between 1972 and 1978. His victims were all young men and boys from the surrounding areas. As the search through the killer's house continued, the policemen found a class ring. Certainly, it didn't belong to Gacy. It belonged to John Szyc.

By the time John, another victim, stepped in the path of the killer clown, Gacy had deployed a long, deadly rally. The friendly man under the funny clothes had faked the community for about six years. After performing at parties, Gacy took off his disguise and removed his makeup to release his cruel real self: the one with a thirst for blood. He would later use his contracting company to recruit young victims, but before, he used to roam the streets as a hunter.

John was 19 years old when he was last seen alive. He was a student and perhaps was looking for a part-time job. He had met Gacy sometime in January 1977. The killer used his company as a trap, offering students attractive jobs. When they were close enough, he used chloroform to drug them and take them to his basement. That was probably the method that Gacy used on January 20 when John vanished and never came back.

Little is known of everything John suffered before dying in Gacy's hands with a rope around his neck. All that is known is that the killer clown tortured and strangled him and later buried the boy's body in the crawl space beneath his house. John was only identified through dental records two years after his disappearance.

Much of Gacy's *modus operandi* was learned from the testimonials of two boys who survived his attacks. One of them, Anthony Antonucci, was only 15 years old when he had to face the horror, lucky enough to escape from the grips of the killer.

Anthony was an employee at Gacy's firm, and one night in July 1975, the macabre clown visited him at his home, knowing his parents were away. The boy couldn't tell if he had been drugged. He could just remember that Gacy persuaded him to watch an adult movie and then managed to wrestle the boy. Gacy was stronger than the boy and overpowered him on the floor. In a quick move, Gacy cuffed Anthony, leaving him incapable of defending himself.

Gacy left the immobilized boy on the ground and walked out of the room for a moment. Just then, Anthony noticed that one of the cuffs was loose and saw an opportunity to escape. He took off the cuffs, and when

Gacy came back, Anthony attacked him. Anthony was a member of the wrestling team at school, and this time, Gacy was the unguarded one.

Nobody could explain why, but that act of courage saved Anthony's life. Perhaps his strength and determination to resist left him out of Gacy's victims' profile. Gacy was impressed by Anthony's reaction and let him go. Yet, Anthony must have been scared and felt threatened until the moment he saw Gacy behind bars. That was when he decided to tell his story for the first time.

It wasn't an act of mercy. Gacy felt no remorse for attacking and killing. He just couldn't handle being challenged and shifting places with the victims. Anthony was an exception to 33 other cases when Gacy accomplished his sinister plan.

Who knows how many he would have killed if Robert Piest's mother hadn't insisted the police go after her child? That night, the detectives didn't stop asking about the smell coming from inside the house—it was the odor of death. The police carried out an exhaustive search throughout the house. Then, they questioned why he had this and that, and all his trash spread on the floor, exposing who he really was. The situation pushed Gacy past his own limit, and he couldn't handle the pressure. He confessed and provided a map detailing where he had buried most of his victims. This map led to the discovery of 26 bodies in the crawl space beneath his home, with additional bodies found on his property and in the Des Plaines River.

Gacy's trial started on February 6, 1980. The prosecution gave their case, and the families of 22 victims spoke. He had confessed to having killed about 30 people, but many of them weren't identified, while some bodies that were found couldn't be related to him. The prosecution shared terrible stories they could rebuild from some witnesses and a survivor of Gacy's attack. The police recovered many personal items belonging to the victims that were displayed during the trial. This caused a deep impression on the jury and the audience since some families recognized their loved ones' properties. Gacy's employees talked about his inappropriate behavior and how he told them to dig in his crawl space. Other witnesses also mentioned Gacy's confession about choking using a "rope trick."

The trial was eerie. Parts of Gacy's house floor, like the trapdoor, were displayed. The medical examiner explained the deaths, showing how brutal Gacy was. Gacy's defense claimed he was mentally ill and brought on the stage specialist who tried to prove he had psychosis episodes. They suggested treatment over jail. They diagnosed Gacy with a personality disorder and argued against temporary insanity during the crimes.

Prosecutor Kunkle challenged the defense on Gacy's premeditation, creating doubt with the jury. Jeffrey Rignall, a survivor, shared his attack story, backing the defense. But his physical reaction while testifying showed the trauma victims suffered, weakening the insanity claim. The prosecutor showed the crimes were premeditated, and he felt no remorse for what he had done. Kunkle used photos of victims to show Gacy's lack of mercy, pushing for a harsh sentence.

After a short deliberation, the jury found Gacy guilty of multiple murders on March 12, 1980. The next day, he received a death sentence. Gacy was taken to Menard Correctional Center, spending 14 years in appeals. Despite claiming innocence at times, he showed no regret, displaying a manipulative attitude throughout. Gacy was executed on May 10, 1994. His last words were, "Kiss my ass".

5

The Jonestown Massacre

Jonestown was a small community located in Guyana, South America. On November 18, 1978, it became the landscape of one of the greatest tragedies and mass massacres in history. It was supposed to be paradise on Earth, but instead, hundreds of people, including women and children, found in it a tragic highway to hell.

That day, 900 people congregated in the Peoples Temple community in Jonestown died after drinking cyanide-laced Kool-Aid in what was alleged to be a collective suicide. Hours of audio tapes demonstrated that even though people ingested the compound voluntarily, they were inducted to take that action by their spiritual leader and their community chief, Jim Jones. What kind of power did this man have to be capable of persuading 900 people to commit suicide? Why would a spiritual leader induce his followers to commit such atrocity?

The Peoples Temple was a religious movement founded in Indianapolis in the late 1950s. Jones was the leader, but for over a decade, the movement remained a branch of the Christian Church (Disciples of Christ), and Jones was an ordained minister. By then, the world was framed by the Cold War, and people feared the outbreak of a nuclear war. In 1965, Jones persuaded his already large congregation to follow him and escape from a nuclear holocaust.

The community settled in Ukiah, California, and the followers engaged in religious and political activities. In the following years, other branches originated in San Francisco and Los Angeles. Jones had ideas about a fairer society. He claimed a community based on mutual cooperation and spiritual values over materialistic objectives. It was the time of the hippie movement's emergence, and speeches calling people to embrace peace and an alternative way of life were very popular. It isn't weird that so many people believed in Jones and didn't hesitate to join his congregation.

In 1974, Jones headed the organization of the agricultural community named Jonestown. Three years later, Jones moved his congregation to Guyana, a small country on the north coast of South America. It is a paradisical tropical land where this community settled to live under their own social rules. It was a utopia, and people came there seeking a peaceful and better life. Even though they thought they were going to the Promised Land, they were, in fact, heading to a torture chamber. The Peoples Temple wasn't a simple community moved by noble ideas but a cult.

Jones, born in Indiana in 1931, had an unusual childhood. He grew up during the Great Depression, a time when many people were poor and struggling. Jones was fascinated by religion from an early age and often attended various churches to observe different practices. His interest in social justice began to grow as he saw the hardships faced by those around him. These early experiences played a significant role in shaping his future endeavors. Nonetheless, his sensitivity toward those who suffered didn't prevent him from taking advantage of their vulnerability.

In the mid-1950s, Jones founded his first church congregation in Indianapolis called the Wings of Deliverance, which was later renamed the Peoples Temple. His goal was to create a congregation that embraced racial integration and helped the underprivileged. This idea was radical at the time, especially in a racially segregated society. Jones's passion for equality attracted like-minded individuals who were eager to support his vision.

But it wasn't just his message that drew people in. Jones possessed an extraordinary charisma that made others feel unique and understood. He knew how to talk to people in a way that made them feel special and important. Many of his followers described feeling an intense connection with him as if he could see into their souls. This ability to connect on a personal level helped him gain a devoted following.

Jones's charisma extended beyond personal interactions. It was evident in his speeches and sermons. He was a powerful speaker, capable of inspiring hope and action among his listeners. He often spoke about love, equality, and justice—themes that resonated deeply with those experiencing social and racial injustices. Through his words, he offered not just spiritual guidance but also a sense of direction and purpose in life.

The religious doctrines within the Peoples Temple were a mix of traditional Christian beliefs and Jones's own interpretations. This commitment to social causes helped solidify the loyalty of many members, as they felt they were part of something greater than themselves.

Jones's rise to prominence was also aided by his strategic use of media and public appearances. His sermons were broadcast on local radio stations, reaching a wider audience and drawing more people to his cause. He also engaged in high-profile activities, such as participating in civil rights marches and organizing community programs, further boosting his visibility and credibility. These efforts showcased his dedication to social justice and reinforced his image as a leader committed to making a positive impact.

Despite his growing influence, there were early signs of his manipulative tendencies. Jones employed various tactics to maintain control over his followers, including emotional manipulation and fear-mongering. He often exaggerated threats from outside forces to create a sense of dependency among his members, convincing them that only he could protect them from harm. This psychological control allowed Jones to wield considerable power over his congregation, even as his public persona remained one of benevolence and compassion.

As the years went by, Jones became increasingly paranoid and controlling. This state of mind was largely why he decided to move the community to Guyana in the first place. As the community grew in members, it was more difficult for Jones to control them and what they said about the Peoples Temple in public. Thus, Jones isolated his followers from their families and the outside world, demanding complete loyalty and obedience. This isolation served to strengthen his influence and prevent dissent within the group. Followers were encouraged to confess their doubts and shortcomings, which Jones would then exploit to reinforce his authority and suppress any challenges to his leadership.

The combination of Jones's charismatic appeal and his authoritative control created a powerful dynamic within the Peoples Temple. Members saw him as both a spiritual guide and a protector—someone who could lead them toward a better future. This duality made it difficult for followers to question his actions or motives, further entrenching his position of power. Nonetheless, Jones knew how to balance his authoritarian leadership style with attending to people's needs.

Life in Jonestown was centered around the concept of communal living, where the residents shared their resources and responsibilities. This lifestyle was heavily promoted by Jones, who believed that a collective approach would ensure everyone's needs were met. The settlement, located in a remote part of Guyana, operated almost like a small village. It consisted of basic wooden structures, including homes, dining areas, and meeting spaces.

Every morning, the community would gather for meetings, often led by Jones himself. These sessions set the tone for the day and reinforced the group's sense of unity. Residents were assigned various tasks to keep the settlement running smoothly. Some worked in agriculture, cultivating crops to feed the community. Others took care of maintenance, keeping the living spaces clean and functional. There were also roles in cooking, nursing, and education, making sure everyone contributed in some way. Everyone felt needed and cherished, and the sense of collectiveness was the main characteristic of the community.

The idea was that everyone worked together for the greater good, embodying the principles Jones preached. Children attended school within the settlement, where they were taught not only regular subjects but also the beliefs of the Peoples Temple. Education played a crucial role in teaching the younger generation about self-sufficiency and loyalty to the community.

Workdays were long and strenuous. From sunrise to sunset, residents were expected to fulfill their duties diligently. Despite the hard work, there was a sense of camaraderie. Shared meals provided opportunities for social interaction, and in the evenings, cultural activities such as music and performances offered some relief from the daily grind. These activities convinced many that they were part of something meaningful.

However, this tight-knit lifestyle came at a cost. One of the significant aspects of life in Jonestown was its isolation from the outside world. The settlement was strategically placed in such a remote location to minimize external influences. Communication with the outside world was strictly monitored. Letters were censored, and visits from outsiders were rare and heavily controlled. This physical and information isolation made it difficult for residents to know what was happening beyond their immediate environment.

Jones used several techniques to maintain this isolation. For instance, he propagated the idea that the outside world was filled with dangers and enemies. He claimed that their community was a sanctuary against a society plagued by racism, corruption, and violence. This narrative fostered fear and suspicion among the residents, making them more reliant on the community and less inclined to seek contact with the outside world.

To reinforce this separation, Jones constructed an elaborate system where he controlled all forms of media within Jonestown. He used loudspeakers to constantly broadcast his sermons and messages, immersing the residents in a flow of ideological content. These broadcasts often included warnings about potential attacks or conspiracies against the Peoples Temple, which heightened the sense of threat from outsiders.

Despite the facade of a caritative and humanistic leader, Jones deployed an authoritarian leadership style, and he demanded absolute devotion from his followers. Through relentless propaganda, Jones positioned himself as a savior figure. He portrayed himself as the only one capable of protecting and guiding the community.

One of his key tactics was the use of public confessionals. During these sessions, individuals were encouraged to confess their doubts and sins in front of the entire community. This tactic served multiple purposes. It acted as a means of social control, as people feared the repercussions of harboring any negative thoughts or dissent. It also created a form of peer pressure, reinforcing the idea that loyalty to Jones was paramount.

Additionally, Jones also implemented different physical and psychological punishments to enforce discipline. Those who disobeyed faced harsh consequences, such as being excluded or beaten. Those who complained about the hard work were forced to work more hours, and children who tried to escape were submersed into the water until they felt they were drowning or were kept in boxes in holes dug into the ground.

Jones also used rewards as part of his strategy. Individuals who displayed extraordinary dedication or zeal were publicly praised and given privileges. Over time, these methods successfully instilled a deep sense of allegiance to Jones and his vision for Jonestown.

Everything seemed to work as Jones had planned. The members of the Peoples Temple community behaved as he expected, either for fear or true conviction. Nonetheless, the effective control Jones had over his community started breaking apart.

Before he moved his community to Guyana, rumors about abusive behaviors within the community had reached the media. One of the reasons why he made the decision to move was to silence those rumors. However, the testimonials about the real living conditions in Jonestown reached the United States, even from distant Guyana.

Some former members of the Peoples Temple had remained in the United States and were concerned about the people living in Jonestown. They were aware of many of the aggressive practices Jones deployed. So, they begged a congressman from California, Leo J. Ryan, to visit Guyana and check for those people's safety.

Ryan and a small entourage reached Jonestown in Guyana in 1978. As they arrived at the community, the state representatives could judge by their own eyes that even though Jones had an effective controlling net that impeded people from leaving if they wanted, most of them were still captivated by the leader's charisma. Yet, Jones was certain that they would come back to the U.S. with relevant information about his habits and abusive power. He realized that the moment he had been preparing for a long time had come.

Jones always thought that despite counting on his community support, people's loyalty could be broken. So, he prepared a final solution to avoid being punished and hold control until the last consequences. He prepared his community for a mass suicide.

He called it the "translation" and spoke about it in his regular sermons through the loudspeakers spread along the community's streets. He told his followers a moment would come when all of them would find death at the same time but only as a step into a new dimension, a purer state of the soul. With their collective death, they would be translated to another planet where they would live forever in a sort of afterlife.

Jones promised a new stage without suffering and endless peace and prosperity, but they had to agree on taking that step, and if they failed to do it as a community, neither of them would enjoy that special pleasure. That meant that all the members of the community had to die at the same time, and as their leader, he trained them for that moment.

The leader usually organized mass suicide drills. He organized public gatherings where a thousand members of the community were ordered to stand up in lines and drink a punch. Every time, they were told that the punch was poisoned and that the moment of the translation had come. People drank, and those who didn't were forced and publicly exposed as those who weren't willing to die with and for the community.

Every time, Jones would later tell them that it had been a simulation to test their faith and commitment to the community. It was the right way to prepare themselves for the moment of the translation that inevitably approached.

Somehow, that moment coincided with the time when the United States government representatives visited Guyana. Before they left, Jones announced the day had come. Ryan and the others were ready to leave Jonestown, but before they boarded the planes, a group of Jones's followers begged them to take them to the U.S. The minute all of them were going to take the plane, some Peoples Temple men opened fire against them. Five people, Ryan among them, were shot. The others had to run to save their lives and hide in the jungle.

Meanwhile, Jones continued with his last deadly ritual. About 1,000 people gathered in the streets and the central square. Jones led the ceremony as usual and told his followers to drink the beverage that would take them to their new life. This time, the beverage was poisoned for real, and it was no drill. The whole ceremony was recorded. Jones's voice encouraged people to drink and make others drink so they could access the afterlife together, as the community they were.

It is uncertain if people followed the instructions because they believed or if there was any external factor that forced them. The 900 bodies were found spread on the ground, one next to another, in groups, in lines, some of them still with a glass in their hand. Some children were still grabbing their mothers' hands, and some others had their legs bent as if they were on their knees while they waited for the translation.

That day, 918 people died, including 300 children. Of them, 909 died after drinking the poisoned punch. The others were either shot or stabbed, but it is unclear who exactly killed them. Jim Jones, the leader of the community, was found dead with a single bullet in his head.

6

David's Demons

David Berkowitz, infamously known as the Son of Sam, terrorized New York City in the 1970s with a spree of violent killings.

It was Christmas Eve, 1975. Some weeks earlier, Berkowitz had written a letter to his father, who lived in Florida. He wrote: "Dad, the world is getting dark now... You wouldn't believe how much some people hate me. Many of them want to kill me... Anyhow, things will soon change for the better" It was an obscure presage of what was about to start.

After that letter, he locked himself in his apartment and wrote disturbing messages on the walls: "In this hole lives the Wicked King. Kill for my Master. I turn children into Killers". Later, Berkowitz told the jury he was tormented by demons which dictated those words and ordered him to kill.

Driven by the demons in his head, Berkowitz roamed the streets of the Bronx while people in the houses got ready to celebrate Christmas. He drove for hours, waiting for the demons to point out the right victim. It was a woman in her early 20s. She had long brown hair, exactly what the demons ordered Berkowitz to look for. She was leaving the grocery store when the demons told Berkowitz that she had to be sacrificed. He got out of the car and approached her with a weapon in his hand. It was a hunting knife. He stabbed her several times and got rid of her body. She was never identified, and the body was never recovered. But that wasn't all that happened that night.

Berkowitz returned to his car and followed the demons' order to keep on searching for another victim. Then, he crossed paths with Michelle Forman, whose life the demons ordered him to take next. And Berkowitz obeyed. He came close to Michelle and took her by her back. He stabbed her with the same knife six times, but Michelle didn't surrender and fought for her life. Eventually, Berkowitz left the body on the street and ran away. Michelle didn't die, but the description she could give of her attacker wasn't enough for the cops to identify him.

Later that night, Berkowitz came back to his apartment, changed his clothes, and apparently, with his demons appeased, he went for a hamburger and fries. When he was captured, the psychiatrists said he was a visionary killer: He believed he was carrying away his crimes as part of a quest assigned by Satan.

Born Richard David Falco, he was given up for adoption shortly after birth and became David Berkowitz when adopted by Pearl and Nathan Berkowitz. His childhood wasn't very different from any ordinary child. His adoptive parents were loving and compassionate, ensuring a stable home. When he was very young, they decided to tell David the truth about his real family. Even though David loved them and was grateful, he couldn't help having feelings of abandonment from his biological mother's rejection. This early emotional wound left a lasting imprint on young David, contributing to a foundation of psychological instability.

As he grew older, this sense of abandonment only intensified. His adoptive mother died of cancer when he was just 14, exacerbating his emotional turmoil. Losing his primary caregiver, who he was deeply attached to, inflicted further psychological pain. This was more than David could deal with. This new trauma sowed seeds of resentment and rage within him, emotions he failed to manage in healthy ways.

After his adoptive mother's death, Nathan, his adoptive father, remarried soon. David's father and his new wife didn't pay much attention to the teen, making him feel sidelined in his own home. This only increased his feelings of isolation and anger.

His early life and feelings of sorrow led other children to bully David at school. They labeled him as a "loner" and frequently teased him. These experiences distorted his worldview, making him see others as sources of potential hurt rather than support, and slowly, he retreated from social circles.

Berkowitz's behavior didn't turn violent overnight—it escalated gradually. Initially, his delinquency manifested in relatively minor activities like arson and petty theft. In his teenage years, he developed an obsession with fire, admitting to setting numerous small fires throughout New York. This fascination hinted at a deeper compulsion to destroy and exert control over a world he perceived as dark and dangerous.

His criminal activities took a more serious turn as he enlisted in the U.S. Army. While there, Berkowitz's behavior began to escalate further. It provided an outlet for his developing aggression and possibly nurtured a more structured form of violence. During those years, he seemed to funnel his extreme emotions through military activities. There, he felt part of a group, feeling respected and included. Nonetheless, when he returned home from service, Berkowitz struggled to reintegrate into civilian life.

He remembered he was alone and nobody cared about him.

Life in the big city has always been challenging, especially for those who struggle to make their own way. Berkowitz was one of them. He grew up in a densely populated, urban environment in New York City, which exposed him to a variety of influences. The city's chaotic and often anonymous atmosphere reinforced his sense of insignificance and detachment.

Furthermore, the cultural milieu of the 1970s—with its rising crime rates and social unrest—may have played a role. Berkowitz's exposure to an environment where violence and fear were increasingly common could have normalized his destructive urges.

Additionally, Berkowitz used to frequent specific neighborhoods where crime was prevalent, which meant he regularly encountered acts of violence and delinquency. These settings potentially reinforced his desensitization to violence and emboldened him to act on his destructive impulses.

In July 1976, Berkowitz was ready to attack again, but this time, he adjusted his *modus operandi*. He wasn't a skillful user of knives, and he had missed when trying to kill his previous victim, so he chose a new weapon. This time, he took a .44-caliber revolver. He had moved out of the Bronx and, therefore, also changed his hunting area.

Berkowitz drove his car with the revolver in his pocket. He searched mainly for young female victims with long dark hair. Eventually, he changed his target to young couples sitting in parked cars near parks or open places. It must have been a new order given by the demons.

Late at night on July 29, 1976, Berkowitz found Donna Lauria, 18 years old, sitting with her friend Jody Valenti in his car. He approached the car and shot at them. Donna died immediately, and Jody was seriously injured. They became Berkowitz's first victims during this malevolent endeavor.

The next day, Berkowitz watched the news and felt proud that his work was in the headlines. He wanted more attention, so with the following attacks, he left a hand-written letter with the victims' bodies. He left encrypted messages with the purpose of puzzling the police and captivating the public. He signed the letters with the pseudonym "the Son of Sam."

Bloody headlines always sell, and the Son of Sam left a rife bloody trace. Berkowitz was a cold-blood killer, but he didn't only want to please dark feelings that grew inside him. He wanted more: He wanted to terrorize as many people as possible, and for that, he used the media. He deployed a strategy to catch the media's attention and amplify fear among the public.

In July 1977, Berkowitz unleashed a killing spree in New York. It lasted less than two years, which was enough time to kill six people and severely wound many others. His first attack didn't end with a fatal victim but encouraged him to perfect his method.

The press played a significant role in amplifying fear among the public. Every new detail about the killings and the cryptic letters Berkowitz sent to the police made headlines. Newspapers used bold, dramatic headlines to capture readers' attention, turning Berkowitz into a household name. This type of reporting increased sales for media companies and fueled a cycle of fear and hysteria. People were gripped by the horror stories they read each morning, which kept them on edge daily. Sensationalized reporting magnified the terror, making it feel as though no one was safe from the Son of Sam.

The extensive coverage of Berkowitz's crimes had both positive and negative effects on the investigation. On the one hand, widespread attention brought more eyes to the case, leading to increased tips from the public. People who saw suspicious activities or individuals were more likely to report them, hoping to end the reign of terror. However, the constant stream of information sometimes hinders law enforcement efforts. False leads and tips flooded in, overwhelming investigators and diverting resources. Additionally, the media frenzy often puts immense pressure on the police to produce quick results, sometimes at the expense of thorough investigations.

The media coverage significantly influenced public perception. During this time, New York City's residents experienced widespread fear and paranoia. People altered their routines, avoiding certain areas and staying indoors after dark. The city's nightlife dwindled, with people feeling unsafe even in their own neighborhoods. The sense of community was disrupted as trust in strangers waned. Reports of the Son of Sam lurking in the shadows of the city led to an atmosphere of suspicion and anxiety.

During the summer of 1977, everybody would talk about the so-called Son of Sam, making his name a household conversation topic. People were afraid but still woke up eager to read the scary details about the killer's crimes and his messages to the police. Letters and encrypted messages were found in the cars where the victims lay dead. Those details were written in bold on the headlines of newspapers and TV shows' "breaking news" banners.

The cops aimed to encourage public opinion to share any information that could help them spot the serial killer; instead, it triggered a scalation of paranoia and an uncontrolled sense of suspicion. Common citizens unconsciously assumed the roles of investigators and tried to discover who the killer was, putting themselves in danger. Moreover, the investigation took the wrong course more than once because people were driven by false leads. The police struggled to separate people's hallucinations from facts that led them to the real killer.

Nonetheless, it was the killer himself who contributed to his capture. Handwriting analysis became instrumental in the investigation. Berkowitz had taken to taunting the police and media with handwritten letters, which provided forensic specialists with samples to scrutinize. Comparing these letters with other documents suspected of being linked to Berkowitz enabled experts to build a profile of his writing style.

The decisive clue that revealed the man behind the name of the Son of Sam was the gun he used to perpetrate his crimes. When investigators discovered that the bullets used in the shootings matched those fired by a 44 caliber Bulldog revolver, information about recent sales of this rare firearm was shared. Cross-referencing sales records against suspect profiles helped to narrow down individuals who had recently acquired such weapons. This meticulous process further pointed to Berkowitz and solidified suspicions surrounding him.

The culmination of these efforts materialized on August 10, 1977, when law enforcement arrested Berkowitz outside his apartment in Yonkers. It marked the end of a reign of terror, bringing relief to a city gripped by fear.

During his trial, Berkowitz was diagnosed as a paranoid schizophrenic, meaning he had a distorted vision of reality. When he was interviewed and asked about his crimes, he confessed and alleged he was following orders from a demon that lived in the neighbor's dog, a giant black Labrador. His neighbor's name was Sam Carr, and Berkowitz said he was referring to that Labrador when he talked about the Son of Sam, the name he used to sign his crimes.

7

Claire Gagnon's Unsolved Murder

Claire Gagnon was 16 years old, and on May 24, 1970, she had gone out with a group of friends, promising her parents she would be back by 5 p.m. to have dinner with them. They all had busy days during the week, so they enjoyed dining together on Sunday evenings. However, that would be a different and tragic Sunday.

Claire grew up in Dieppe—a small, tight-knit community in New Brunswick, Canada. Neighbors loved her because she was friendly and considerate to everybody. Her life was filled with rich interactions and daily routines that painted a picture of normalcy. She had a stable job, close relationships with her family, and an active social life.

The town she lived in was relatively peaceful, making the events that unfolded all the more shocking. Families had lived there for decades, so they knew each other well, and there seemed to be nothing to be afraid of. People left their doors unlocked, and it was usual to find children playing in the front yard after dinner. Streets and common areas were quiet and safe. To Claire's parents, it wasn't unusual for the teenager to return home on her own.

That Sunday was May 24, and Claire's parents weren't immediately worried when the clock showed it was already 5:00 p.m. and their daughter hadn't returned. She was surely having fun with her friends. However, as time passed by, they started to wonder why she wouldn't have phoned home to let them know she would come back later. That behavior wasn't typical for Claire: She only went out after asking her parents and would always let them know wherever she went and whoever she was with.

When Claire didn't show up by 9 a.m., her parents really began to worry. It was evident that something was wrong. Claire's parents called all her friends and those who could know anything about the girl. Nobody could tell where she was.

Claire's parents went to the police and explained their daughter was missing. The first answer was that she was probably still hanging around with her friends. The police said they couldn't go after every teenager who didn't come home on time. It was a very discouraging answer for the couple. They decided to start searching on their own.

Claire's parents called their neighbors and organized informal search groups. They also phoned everybody who knew Claire. Nobody had seen her or heard about her. Her friends said she was with them early in the day, but she left before 2 p.m. She had told them her parents would be waiting for her. That is all the information they could gather.

Later that night, the police became involved in the search. The local authorities launched search efforts to find her. Local law enforcement teamed up with volunteer groups to scour the surrounding areas. They searched meticulously trails, parks, and even abandoned buildings while trying to find any clues that could lead them to Claire. Within a few hours, the police also distributed flyers with Claire's photo and description. Her friends and family remained hopeful, participating actively in every search mission and rallying community support.

In reviewing Claire's life, investigators looked for any warning signs or red flags that might suggest trouble. They examined her relationships, both personal and professional, and sifted through her digital footprint. Friends and family were interviewed extensively. Some noted that Claire had recently received unsettling messages from an unknown number, though she brushed them off as prank calls. Others mentioned that Claire had been feeling slightly uneasy over the past few weeks, though she attributed it to stress due to her exams at school.

Both investigators and families had turned from hope to desperation. New specialized teams, including those with cadaver dogs, joined the investigation. The whole neighborhood was consternated because they knew what was implicit. Community members continued to assist, organizing search parties and keeping Claire's story alive in the media, though they had the sense that the objective of the search had turned from finding Claire alive to finding her body.

Then came a breakthrough: 24 hours after Claire's disappearance that Sunday, a group of investigators found a body. It was a female teenager. The difficult terrain and dense foliage had made the site virtually inaccessible, and this had prevented people from finding her earlier. Law enforcement agencies converged on the scene, securing it for a detailed forensic examination. The autopsy revealed the girl was a victim of homicide.

Claire's parents were called to recognize the body, and sadly, they confirmed that the body that lay lifeless on the stretcher in the freezing room was their daughter. The police explained to the family that she was lying on the ground in a field only 300 yards away from her house when a group found her. She had a rope around her neck and signs of violence. It was evident she had been strangled. Some people later said it was, in fact, an electrical wire. She also had a towel inside her mouth, which suggested the aggressor had tortured her before killing her. The discovery, while heartbreaking, provided some closure to her loved ones. But questions still loomed. Who could have done such a thing? And why?

Family and friends couldn't think of anybody who could have possibly wanted to hurt Claire. She had no enemies. It was a small town with a population of nearly 4,000 inhabitants, and everybody knew each other. Nobody had seen a stranger or suspicious person wandering the area. Was it possible that the killer was among the neighbors who had known Claire since she was a child?

After Claire's death, the police opened an investigation to find out who had killed her. One of the first significant steps in the investigation involved gathering physical evidence from the crime scene. Investigators meticulously combed through the area where Claire's body was found, looking for anything that might provide a clue. They collected fibers, hair samples, and any potential weapons. Each item was carefully cataloged and sent to a forensic lab for analysis. The only significant pieces of evidence found in the place were the wire and the towel used to suffocate Claire. Nothing was found in her clothes or beneath her fingernails, which suggested she couldn't defend herself from her aggressor.

Despite the forensic specialists' efforts, DNA tests to evidence pieces didn't bring any clear data about what happened or who had hurt Claire. The forensic analysis included comparing DNA found at the scene with samples from known individuals. Additionally, fingerprint analysis was conducted on any surfaces where prints might have been left. Investigators hoped to identify potential suspects or witnesses, but nothing worked. There were no matches between the DNA found in the crime scene and the list of criminals in the area.

Key witnesses were another vital aspect of the investigation. Law enforcement interviewed numerous individuals who knew Claire or had seen her in the days leading up to her death. Among these were friends, family members, schoolmates, and neighbors. Each witness offered pieces of information that helped build a timeline of events. Their accounts varied, some providing detailed recollections while others only remembered minor details. Every bit of information was considered important, as it could lead to a breakthrough in understanding what happened. In the end, each new testimonial opened a new investigation line that led nowhere and diversified the efforts. Instead of contributing to solving the tragic mystery, each new clue pushed the investigators away further from the truth.

The only confirmed fact was that Claire was last seen alive that tragic Sunday between 2 and 3 p.m. near the area where she was found dead. Witnesses didn't see anybody else around and couldn't remember any detail about Claire that could suggest she felt in danger. Everyone seemed to point out she was just going home to meet her parents.

Despite their best efforts, law enforcement encountered various hurdles during the investigation. One significant challenge was the passage of time. As months and years went by without a resolution, critical evidence deteriorated or was lost. Witnesses' memories faded, and potential leads grew cold. The case never reached the frontlines of the national press. Only the local media covered the news of a teenager found dead in a small town where nothing ever happened. While media coverage is usually helpful to keep the spot on the case, most times, it leads to misinformation or sensationalism, adding pressure on investigators and influencing witnesses' willingness to come forward. In this case, it made little difference.

Maintaining public interest and the community's cooperation with the police was difficult, making it harder to collect new information. As public interest declined, another obstacle arose: a lack of sufficient resources. Comprehensive investigations require substantial funding, manpower, and expertise. Budgetary constraints often limit the scope of what could be done.

Years passed, and Claire's case remained unsolved. Since there was no progress in the investigation, the police stopped looking for the killer, and it became a cold case. The only lead to the potential killer was in 1993 when the police filed a case against a man they believed had committed the crime. Later, it was proven that the man was in a mental health hospital when Claire was murdered. The case went cold again.

Throughout these trying times, Claire's family fought to keep her memory alive, advocating for justice and ensuring that her case remained in the public eye. Public vigils and memorials were held, offering communal spaces for grief and solidarity.

Despite their efforts, critical leads went cold, and the lack of concrete evidence made it difficult to identify a clear suspect. The discovery of Claire's body brought some closure, yet it also intensified the need for answers about who was responsible and why this tragedy occurred. Claire's death remains unsolved, and the police aren't looking for her killer any longer. Can we say justice did everything they could to find the truth? Perhaps, but the monster who took her life, probably someone from her close circle, walks freely on the same streets as Claire's family and people who still mourn for her.

8

The Yorkshire Ripper

Why would a teenager prefer to spend time roaming cemeteries instead of partying with their friends? When Peter was an adolescent, he used to visit graveyards on his own and would spend hours wandering among the tombstones. It wasn't typical behavior.

As time passed by, those odd behaviors aggravated and became more and more frequent. He withdrew socially and developed an unusual fascination with death and the macabre. This early fixation on death and mortality might have been an escape from his tumultuous home life but also served as a precursor to his future heinous acts. No one could predict that it was the beginning of a dark path that would lead him to the killing spree that earned him an infamous name: Yorkshire Ripper.

On a warm and dry afternoon in September 1969, Peter went on a ride with his friend Trevor in his minivan. Trevor was driving and decided to pull over for a moment. It was just getting dark. Peter jumped out of the minivan without saying a word and left. He walked down a street along a neighborhood of terraced houses, with a church standing at the end. Later, Peter would say it was an accusing finger addressing the sinners.

Peter approached a woman who was standing in the corner, near the wall. He picked a rock from the street and put it into a sock. Then, he asked the woman what time it was, and before she could answer, he clubbed her in the head with the rock in the sock. The strike was so hard that the sock broke, and the woman fell on the sidewalk, bleeding abundantly. Peter believed he had killed her. He turned around and ran to his friend's minivan.

It had only taken ten minutes for Peter to have his first recorded victim. When he reached the van, he was sweating and breathing heavily. Trevor thought he had been robbed, but as he entered the vehicle, he told Trevor he had taken revenge on a sex worker because she had cheated him of some money. He was frantic. He had finally released all the rage he hosted inside.

Many years later, he explained he didn't follow a special pattern or spend a long time choosing his victims. Instead, he believed prostitutes were responsible for his troubles, and somehow, he wanted to punish them. Therefore, he would just go out to the streets and attack any sex worker he found.

The pattern of behavior exhibited by Peter Sutcliffe before he became known as the Yorkshire Ripper provides a chilling look into the progression and escalation of his violence over time. Initially, much of his aggression and hostility were internalized or expressed through minor criminal acts.

However, a pivotal moment came in 1969 when Peter was arrested for fraud after being caught with stolen goods. Although this encounter didn't directly hint at his violent potential, it was a sign that he had begun engaging in criminal activities. The authorities failed to delve deeper into his psychological state or recognize any underlying issues that could escalate into more severe offenses. Violence was, however, awakened at a very early age.

Peter Sutcliffe was born in 1946 in Bingley, West Yorkshire. He experienced a childhood marked by several traumatic events. He grew up in a working-class family, but life at home didn't feel safe and happy.

Sutcliffe's upbringing was far from stable or nurturing. His father, John Sutcliffe, was a domineering figure who exhibited aggressive behavior toward his children. At home, Peter witnessed frequent arguments between his parents, which often turned violent. This chaotic environment likely contributed to feelings of insecurity and resentment that Peter carried into adulthood. Furthermore, Peter's mother, Kathleen, although more empathetic, struggled to shield her son from his father's wrath, contributing to an inconsistent emotional support system.

He was still very young when he had his first encounters with law enforcement. His initial brushes with the law were relatively minor and didn't raise immediate red flags. For instance, during his teenage years, Peter was caught committing petty thefts, but these incidents were either overlooked or resulted in minimal consequences. It wasn't until the mid-1970s that these violent fantasies began materializing into physical violence against women.

Sutcliffe's transition from fantasies to actual violence started with acts of animal cruelty, a common trait observed in many serial killers. Torturing animals allowed him to practice inflicting pain and death without immediate repercussions. Soon after, Sutcliffe escalated to attacking women, initially targeting sex workers whom he believed wouldn't be missed by society.

As years went by, Sutcliffe's methods became more brutal and calculated. He developed a specific *modus operandi*, often using hammers and knives, intending to inflict maximum pain and ensure his victims' deaths. Each attack followed a similar pattern, highlighting his growing confidence and the increased savagery of his actions. His ability to evade capture for so long speaks volumes about the shortcomings in investigative techniques and a failure to understand or profile such escalating behavior adequately.

After his first ride that evening with his friend, Sutcliffe continued to lurk for women on the streets. On October 30, 1975, he would claim his first fatal victim. She was Wilma McCann, a 28-year-old woman and mother of four children. Although she wasn't a sex worker, a night at the clubs in the city center put her on the killer's path.

She left her children with their nanny and told them to go to bed early. She was going out with some friends. She couldn't have known that when she closed her house door at around 7:30 p.m., it would be the last time her children saw her. She went to the center of Chapeltown and visited some pubs. At some point in the evening, Sutcliffe stopped his car by Wilma and invited her for a ride. She probably accepted.

The next day, Wilma was found dead in Prince Philip Playing Fields, a few blocks away from her house. Sutcliffe had struck her at the back of her head twice with a hammer before stabbing her with a knife 15 times.

Sutcliffe was determined to kill. He prepared himself to kill. His attack on Wilma wasn't the first one with more lethal weapons than simply a rock in a sock. In July

1975, Sutcliffe attacked a woman named Anna Rogulskyj in Keighley, West Yorkshire. People in the area knew her as Irish Annie, and she was 42 at the moment of the aggression. She was walking home on a Friday night.

Sutcliffe attacked her in the street and struck her with a hammer. Then, he slashed at her abdomen with a knife. He left, leaving the body in a pool of blood. A young boy who was passing by found her on the ground early the next morning. She was still breathing. Despite the severity of the attack, Anna survived, but the police didn't connect this incident to Sutcliffe.

In August 1975, Sutcliffe attacked his next victim in Halifax: Olive Smelt. Similar to previous assaults, he used a hammer and knife, leaving Olive critically injured. She survived but with lasting physical and psychological scars. In both cases, the descriptions provided by the survivors bore similarities, but the police failed to link these attacks conclusively.

Even though the police weren't even close to identifying Sutcliffe as the killer, he improved his attacks and took more care to cover his trace. On September 1, 1979, the Yorkshire Ripper committed one of his most violent and carefully deployed attacks. He killed the 11th of the 13 women in his record—those were, at least, the women proven to be his victims.

The next victim was Barbara Leach. She was 20 years old and studied social psychology at Bradford University. She had gone out with friends—apparently, a type of behavior for women that Sutcliffe wanted to punish—and was walking home alone. She was alone, and it was dark, but she always walked home on her own. That night, someone was hiding and waiting for her. It was Sutcliffe.

When she stepped by him, he took her by her back and dragged her to an alleyway. There, he stabbed her to death with a knife. This time, he hid the body that would be found two days later. The police were looking for her after her friends reported her missing.

The succession of attacks in 1975 alerted the authorities, and a manhunt began. However, it took seven years for the police to connect the crimes and have enough clues as to who the Yorkshire Ripper could be.

One significant challenge faced by the police was the geographical spread of Sutcliffe's crimes. Northern England encompasses a vast area with varied terrain and multiple jurisdictions. For instance, investigators in West Yorkshire had to liaise continuously with their counterparts in Greater Manchester, Leeds, and other areas where Sutcliffe struck, leading to logistical complexities and delays.

Moreover, the decentralized system meant that information about potential suspects and witness statements were scattered across different departments.

The lack of a unified database for tracking suspects or pooling clues made it easier for Sutcliffe to escape detection.

The forensic science available at the time also significantly limited the investigation. Techniques such as DNA profiling, which are standard practice today, did not exist during the initial stages of the Yorkshire Ripper case. Forensic capabilities for scrutinizing crime scenes were primitive. Essential evidence like fibers, hair samples, and residues might have been overlooked or improperly handled due to the limited understanding of their significance. The tools and expertise to analyze such evidence accurately had not yet evolved, thereby hampering the ability to build a concrete case against Sutcliffe early on.

The brutal nature of the murders attracted extensive media coverage, which often sensationalized details and fueled public panic. The involvement of the press led to widespread fear and speculation, creating an environment of urgency and chaos. Newspapers frequently published speculative articles that sometimes conflicted with ongoing investigative efforts, potentially compromising sensitive information and misleading the public.

One notable blunder involved a victim who survived an attack and provided a description that closely matched Sutcliffe's appearance. However, senior officers dismissed the attack as unrelated to the Ripper series, directing resources away from Sutcliffe. This dismissal likely delayed his capture and allowed him to continue his crime spree.

Additionally, the policy of eliminating suspects based on non-definitive criteria, such as accent or handwriting alone, proved detrimental. Various suspects, including Sutcliffe, were wrongly dismissed due to inconsistent application of elimination policies. Eventually, the arrest of Peter Sutcliffe, notorious as the Yorkshire Ripper, marked a pivotal moment in the history of British criminal investigations.

On the night of January 2, 1981, routine police patrol officers Robert Hydes and Sergeant Robert Ring spotted a car with false number plates. Upon investigating further, they found Sutcliffe in the vicinity, who gave a flimsy explanation for his presence there. This encounter resulted in Sutcliffe's arrest based on suspicion of stolen property. During his detention, Sutcliffe was strip-searched, revealing that he wore an inverted jumper under his trousers, which resembled a type of crude body armor. This discovery, combined with the concealment of weapons such as a hammer and knife, escalated the investigation into his possible involvement in graver crimes.

Further probing uncovered more incriminating evidence. Sutcliffe eventually admitted to being the

Yorkshire Ripper during a police interview, confessing to the murders. These revelations confirmed suspicions and helped solidify the case against him.

The courtroom drama surrounding Sutcliffe's trial was filled with tension and high stakes. His trial began on May 5, 1981, at the Old Bailey in London, presided over by Mr. Justice Boreham. The prosecution, led by Attorney General Sir Michael Havers and Harry Ognall, presented compelling arguments against Sutcliffe. They depicted him as a calculated and sadistic murderer. However, the defense team introduced medical evidence suggesting that Sutcliffe suffered from paranoid schizophrenia. According to the psychiatrist brought by the defense, Sutcliffe claimed he was driven by divine commands to kill prostitutes, referring to his actions as a "mission."

The court faced the dilemma of deciding whether Sutcliffe's mental state significantly impaired his responsibility for the murders. The jury had to weigh the conflicting narratives presented by both sides and evaluate the evidence that surfaced showing Sutcliffe might have been attempting to deceive the psychiatrists. On multiple occasions, he was heard saying he could avoid a long prison sentence by feigning insanity.

Ultimately, the jury found Sutcliffe guilty of murder on all counts. He received twenty consecutive life sentences, though he was confined at Broadmoor Hospital, a high-security psychiatric facility, which became a period of both containment and controversy. While incarcerated, Sutcliffe remained a figure of public infamy, and his life behind bars was scrutinized heavily by the media. However, his explanations about what motivated his attacks didn't prove he was insane. On the contrary, his words showed he knew how much damage he caused. He said, "The voices told me it wasn't good enough just to attack them. I had to do it properly. I had to kill".

9

The Schoolboy Murders in Sydney

The 1970s schoolboy murders in Sydney stand as one of the most harrowing series of crimes in Australia's history. The fear and grief that enveloped the city still resonate today. This period saw young lives cut short under brutal circumstances, leaving a permanent scar on their families and the entire community.

In 1976, Stephen was a student at Enmore Boys High School. Daily life wasn't very different from any other high school. Some teenagers became friends and comrades, while others became rivals. Stephen and his family didn't imagine that school could be a dangerous place. When the schoolboys were found dead, it was impossible to know that the one to blame walked through school corridors and was nearly the same age as his victims.

Stephen was lucky enough to be attacked at his school when some of his friends were close enough to help him. They were outside, in the playground. Stephen and other students were going to a building to grab items for their next class. He was taking some tools and doing woodwork when he felt extreme pain in his back. He didn't know what was going on.

He screamed in pain and turned to see that he had been attacked by one of his mates. His name was Mark Gregory, a typical 17-year-old adolescent with a colossal strength and a disturbing willingness to hurt people. He had taken Stephen from his shoulders and placed his knee at the middle of the spine, making the unprevented boy bend in pain.

At the moment, Stephen didn't realize, but many years later, looking back at that moment, he knew that Gregory knew exactly where to push to inflict the most pain. Stephen was lucky that Gregory didn't have the chance to go further. Other boys faced a tragically different destiny.

Sometime after the episode at the high school playground, the police came when they were in class and arrested Gregory. He was accused of sexually assaulting and killing two schoolboys. Stephen wasn't Gregory's first victim, though with others, he had been far more cruel.

While he pretended to have a normal life, he perpetrated terrible crimes.

Garry John Bakemeyer was 12 years old and loved going to school. He lived with his mother at the Elsie Women's Refuge in Glebe, Sydney. Everybody said he was a good student and a charming boy with dreams and aspirations. His mother was very proud of him.

On the afternoon of Friday, July 9th, 1976, Garry was with his friend, a younger child. They were playing at Doctor Foley's Rest Park when a young man approached them. He had short brown hair and was dressed in casual clothes. He was wearing grey trousers and a yellow sweater. This man was, of course, Gregory, but instead of attacking the children as he did with Stephen, he used a different, more deliberate strategy.

The aggressor first made a move to earn the children's trust and take them away from the park. He wanted to drive them where no one could see. He told the boys he would give them some money if they helped him carry some boxes. The kids agreed and left with him. When they asked where the boxes were, the stranger told them they were at Jubilee Oval.

Once there, the stranger told the younger boy to wait there while Garry and he took care of the boxes. The young boy made him promise he would also have a box because he also wanted to earn some money. Gregory agreed and left with Garry. The aggressor took the boy out of his friend's sight to a viaduct near the train lines.

Shortly after, the stranger came back alone and told the young boy that his friend had finished his part of the job and had already gone home. The boy was disappointed because he had made no money and his friend had left him alone. He eventually went home.

On Sunday, July 11, Garry's mother went to the police station and reported her son missing. He hadn't returned home on Friday or Saturday. He seemed to have vanished. She had gone to the police on Friday night, but they didn't take the report. On Monday, Garry's friend told his mother that Garry hadn't gone to school, and the woman phoned the police to inform them. It was clear that something was wrong.

The police officers interviewed Garry's young friend, who told them about the man who had intercepted them in the park. The child told the story about the boxes and the money and went with the investigators to the place where he had seen Garry for the last time. The police left the child with his mother and came back to Jubilee Oval.

It didn't take long for the police to reach a disheartening scene. They found a body, evidently of a young boy. He was just a child. He had his clothes torn and his small and fragile body brutally beaten. It was evident that he had been abused and the victim of a ferocious attack. Who could have done such a hideous crime?

It was proven that the victim was Garry. His young friend made a great contribution to the case by providing details about the aggressor, but still, the police weren't sure who was responsible for the crime.

Months passed by, and a new school year was about to start. Stephen was hopeful to think that he wouldn't meet Gregory at school again because he had dropped out. Nonetheless, he would still find Gregory on his way when he returned the following year. Stephen didn't know that he was witnessing the moment when he picked his next victim.

It was a hot day in January of 1977, and kids were coming back to school after the summer holidays. Stephen was walking down the front stairs of Enmore Boys High School when he saw a disturbing and familiar figure on the other side of the street. Gregory was with a boy who seemed to be much younger and smaller in size. Gregory was talking avidly to the child. Even though Stephen felt distressed to see Gregory again, he didn't think the boy could be in danger. He walked away but noticed that Gregory led the boy to Enmore Park.

The boy with Gregory was Wayne Spencer Nixon. He was 12 years old and was still in primary school. He was about to start his first year at Newtown High School. Every day, Wayne took the brown and white colored private bus line, the same that Stephen took, to go to school. But one morning during that January, Wayne didn't take the bus.

It was 6 p.m. on January 31, 1976, when the phone at the ATN Channel Seven rang. An anonymous male voice asked to talk to the time prime newscaster, Roger Climpson. He said he had a scoop. The newscaster was busy and couldn't take the call, so the anonymous informer phoned again. This time, he revealed that there was a dead body in Jubilee Oval, right at the same place where Garry was killed.

Climpson didn't believe the caller, but still, he informed the police. When they went to check, they found another body, again of a young boy. The body was placed at the same spot where Garry was, also with his face to the ground, his clothes broken, and signs of severe physical violence. The forensic specialists later revealed the time of the death. The boy was killed in the park on Sunday afternoon while a crowd was around playing cricket or walking with their dogs. Nobody heard a sound.

The crime scene was sealed to keep the curious away, and the body was taken to the morgue. There, the specialists carried out the autopsy and determined that the body, besides being assaulted, had been stabbed several times in his legs and arms. What killed him was a stab in his chest. The killer used a 12.5-long knife that reached to his heart and drilled it. The knife was later found in a rubbish bin and played an important role in gathering evidence.

What had happened to Wayne? The events were reconstructed from the testimonials of the people who last saw him. His mother said that Wayne left home that Sunday morning to swim in Leichhardt Municipal Pool. Then, he had lunch with his family and left again. He rode his bike to a friend's house, but he didn't find anyone at home.

Later that afternoon, a neighbor saw Wayne with another guy riding his bike. The neighbor described the guy as a bit older than Wayne, with short brown hair. He said Wayne didn't look scared or in trouble. On the contrary, he waved and said goodbye. The unknown guy was no other but Gregory. They had met that Sunday morning at the pool. Gregory told Wayne to meet him in the afternoon with a pretext similar to the one he used to take Garry. Unfortunately, Wayne also trusted the stranger too quickly.

The police immediately connected both crimes. The age of the victims was the same, and the position of the bodies and the damage caused to them were signs of the same procedure. Then, the testimonials about the young man seen in the company of the victims revealed that the aggressor was the same one.

The police were looking for more evidence, including the weapon and Wayne's bicycle. His mother had given it to him for his last birthday. That Sunday afternoon, Wayne was riding his bike, and it wasn't with the body at Jubilee Oval. Instead, it was found days later in the Parramatta River at Iron Cove, about 1.25 miles from the place where Wayne's body was. While it was evident that the bike had been discharged, witnesses described a different guy riding the bike after Sunday afternoon. It didn't shed any light on the case.

One of the key testimonials came from Stephen's mother. She was waiting for the bus that fatal Sunday when she saw Wayne with an older guy, walking with the child's bike at his side. She heard when Gregory told the boy to hurry up as if he was in a rush. She didn't know, but they were heading to Jubilee Oval in Glebe, the place where Gregory had planned to kill Wayne.

At first, Stephen's mother didn't realize that the assassinated boy on the news was the same boy she had seen that afternoon. A few weeks later, Stephen and his mother were at the city center when they met Gregory. Stephen had a small conversation with him, and then, his mother recognized him as the guy with the child and the bike that afternoon, but still couldn't connect the scene with the later crime.

After house-by-house research, the police eventually found out that the schoolboys' killer was Mark Gregory. They found incriminating evidence at his house, and the many testimonials they gathered coming from people who identified him in identikits drawn by specialists were enough to raise charges against him.

By March 1977, the police knew that Gregory had killed those children. Even though Gregory was imprisoned, justice had to wait until his 18th birthday in March 1978 to judge and condemn him for double homicide. It took a very short time for the jury to reach a sentence.

He was sentenced to two consecutive life sentences. The defense aimed to obtain a reduction in the sentence and the right to parole since he was under the age of 18 when he committed the crimes. They alleged that he needed psychiatrist attention. Nonetheless, the jury remained firm in their decision and alleged that he had shown no mercy to his victims; thus, he deserved at least equal treatment, and no mercy would be shown to him. He should never leave prison so he would never have a chance to hurt another boy again.

10

Gary Allan Srery— Canada's Lesser-Known Monster

Gary Allan Srery, a name not widely known in the annals of criminal history, left an ominous legacy in Calgary. His actions involved taking the lives of four women and girls, casting a long shadow over their families and the community. Each victim's story is marked by sorrow and tragedy, offering a glimpse into the devastating consequences of his crimes.

Eva Dvorak was 14 years old. She was a student at Ian Bazalgette Junior High, where she had many friends. Sometimes, she got in trouble because she was a bit rebellious, but she was a kind girl, loved by her parents and sisters.

One Friday, she went to school as usual. There, she met her best friend, Patsy McQueen, and had the bad idea of hiding from their teachers and drinking a beer. When they didn't attend their classes, an assistant searched for them. They caught the girls in the middle of their prank and took them to the headmistress' office. They had committed a major offense at school, and so they were sent home. They were supposed to come back on Monday with their parents.

Eva and Patsy left school at noon. They didn't feel well because they had been drinking. They headed to their homes and walked down 12th Street and 9th Avenue S.E. That was the place where they were last seen alive. The girls didn't make it home that Friday, February 13, 1976.

The girls' families and friends looked for them and reported them as missing. The police hadn't started searching yet when a man from Calgary found two bodies. On Sunday morning, he was driving along Highway 1 toward his properties in the west of the city. He noticed something unusual and approached to inspect.

The two girls were lying on the ground a few yards down the highway in the Happy Valley Recreation Centre (the present-day community of Valley Ridge). The man immediately called the police, and soon, the bodies were identified as the missing girls.

Nobody could bring any information about where the girls had been between Friday at noon and Sunday morning. The autopsy revealed that the girls were already dead when the killer left the bodies at that place, probably trying to hide them. They were certainly murdered somewhere else.

The girls' homicide was a complete mystery. Their clothes were untouched, and there were no signs of stress on their bodies. They hadn't been sexually abused and had no clear evidence of the causes of their deaths. The killer didn't shoot or stab them, and there were no signs of suffocation. Yet, the authorities discharged the hypothesis of death by exposure. The weather conditions and the time that had passed by weren't enough to cause the death of the teenagers. The autopsy revealed they had taken alcohol and drugs but couldn't determine if that caused their deaths.

Without any testimonials and lacking data about the causes of death, the investigation to find the aggressor became almost impossible. Nobody had seen the girls. Even people at Ian Bazalgette Junior High, they hesitated to affirm that the girls had attended school on Friday. The investigation had plenty of blank spaces.

For a long time, the investigation stagnated, and the police were about to declare it a cold case. Then, a new crime was connected with the teenagers' murder. On September 16, 1976, another girl's body was found. She was Melissa Ann Rehorek, 20 years old.

Melissa was originally from Windsor and had recently moved to Calgary for work. She had been hired as a housekeeper. Her family described her as an adventurous young woman who enjoyed traveling, with many friends and people who loved her. She was last seen on the evening of September 15, 1976. She was going hiking outside the city, and a transit driver told the police he had dropped her on the Trans-Canada Highway, not far from the place where her body was found. The predator might have intercepted her as she walked by the road.

The killer had left her body in a ditch about 12.4 miles west of Calgary. The predator had dug along the road and thrown the body of the woman who was already dead. According to the police, the killer abducted the victims and killed them somewhere else.

Like the others, the young woman's clothes were unripped. On this occasion, the police could establish the cause of death. Melissa had been strangled. There were signs of suffocation and marks around her neck. The police also discovered signs of struggle that made them believe she had fought for her life or that she didn't know her aggressor. Thus, he forced the girl to take her with him in the abduction. Hair, human skin remains, and pieces of what could be clothing were found under Melissa's fingernails, yet the police couldn't use them to track the killer.

In the 1970s, forensic sciences weren't as developed as they are today, and there wasn't much evidence with relevant information at the time. Nonetheless, the Calgary investigation groups did a meticulous job gathering evidence from the bodies and the crime scenes.

In the case of Melissa, the investigators found fluids in her body that could be of her aggressor. Since DNA tests weren't yet available, there was no way to use that data to capture the killer. However, many years later, the case of Melissa was reopened, and the police used that information to charge Gary Allen Srery. He was already paying a life sentence for a sexual offense at the Idaho State Prison.

This evidence not only provided leads in her case but also helped link him to other potential crimes. The findings brought some semblance of closure to her family, though the ache of loss remained profound. Her case underscored the importance of vigilance and the role technology plays in solving modern-day crimes.

The DNA discoveries about Melissa's death and her aggressor helped clarify Eva's and Patsy's crimes. While at the time, the police couldn't prove whether they had been abused or not, this new evidence set the stage for a new hypothesis. The cases were also reopened, and new tests allowed the police to connect the crimes and establish the killer's *modus operandi*.

Eventually, they found a fourth victim, who Srery had also killed. The victim was a 19-year-old girl named Barbara James MacLean. Her death had many points in common with the other three girls killed in Calgary.

Barbara was a physician's daughter from Nova Scotia and was away from her family home for the first time. She had recently moved to Calgary to work in a bank. On the night of February 25, 1977, she went to a bar called the Highlander Hotel Tavern with some friends and her boyfriend. The people who were with her told later the police Barbara had an argument with her boyfriend. It was late, and everybody was getting ready to leave, but Barbara was angry and decided to go home alone. Her friends saw her for the last time at about 2:00 a.m.

The next morning, a man was walking with his dog by 80th Avenue and 6th Street N.E. when he saw a body lying by the road. Again, the killer had dropped the victim's body beside a gravel road. Like the other three girls, Barbara's clothes were on and unharmed, though her jacket was inside out. She had also been strangled, and there were signs of violence.

On this occasion, the police could also gather enough evidence from Barbara's body. After interrogating and scrutinizing all of Barbara's friends, family, and boyfriend, the authorities reached the conclusion they were all clean. She didn't have any enemies, so there was no initial suspect for this crime.

A witness affirmed to have seen her walking through 16th Avenue, where the bar was located, and then getting into a cab. Thus, the police obtained samples of 600 cab drivers and interviewed hundreds of others. The testimonials didn't provide any further details to clarify who killed Barbara, and the samples couldn't be properly contrasted with those found in the girl's body. Nonetheless, Barbara's father, a man of science, predicted that his daughter's murder would be solved when genetics and technology developed.

The Herald, a local newspaper, published Barbara's murder and the stories of many other girls who had been assassinated between 1975 and 1977 in the same area. There were many similarities between the victims' profiles and the crime scenes. However, it wasn't until 2021 that the police revised the cases. Then, equipped with more developed technology, they could connect the cases, identify the aggressor, and trace him.

Gary Allan Srery was a U.S. citizen who reached Canada in the middle 1970s, the period of his killing raids. In the 1960s, he had been convicted of kidnapping and sex offenses in the U.S., but somehow, he was free. For many decades, he remained unnoticed and dodged the authorities in Canada until, in 1999, he was found guilty of sexual assault and sent back to the United States to serve a five-year sentence.

He never stopped committing the same crimes. When the police could match Srery's DNA with the Calgary victims' aggressor, he was serving a life sentence in Idaho for the same charges. He died in 2011, many years before the Calgary cases were solved.

The victims' lives had certain things in common that placed them on the killer's list—they had something he sought to calm his fury. They all followed a similar path that led them to a fatal ending. Each victim had unique circumstances that led them to cross paths with this predator, and the police couldn't prove if any of the many other victims in those years in Calgary were also Srery's work.

Analyzing the crime scenes tied to each victim reveals common patterns in Srery's methodology. He often chose locations that were less monitored, making it easier for him to evade capture initially.

Srery's criminal background in the United States before illegally crossing into Canada suggests a readiness and capability to commit similar atrocities elsewhere. His extensive record of rapes and kidnappings in the United States during the 1960s underlines his dangerous tendencies. The fact that he changed his appearance, vehicles, and names frequently implies he was adept at evading law enforcement, making it plausible that he could have committed crimes in other countries without detection. Although Canadian authorities have pieced together some fragments of his timeline, large gaps remain, particularly from the mid-1970s until his arrest in the 1990s.

Unresolved mysteries around Srery's activities continue to haunt investigators and the affected communities. Beyond the confirmed homicides in Calgary, there are suspicions surrounding other crimes that Srery may have been involved in. These unresolved cases present significant challenges due to various factors, including a lack of means to interpret physical evidence, witnesses, and the passage of time, which deteriorate the chances of solving them.

Theories and speculations about what motivated Srery's unsolved activities abound. While his known crimes suggest patterns of sexual assault and murder, entirely understanding his motivations is difficult without direct testimony or psychological evaluation. Some speculate he was driven by deep-seated psychological issues and past experiences, while others consider the possibility of opportunistic behavior honed by years of criminal activity. The police could only reconstruct Srery's cruel *modus operandi*. He would lurk his victims behind the wheel of his car, attack them from behind, and force them into his car. Then, he would assault them and strangle them before dropping their bodies beside the road as if he expected them to be found.

The emotional toll on victims' families and the broader community cannot be overstated. Unresolved cases leave families without closure, perpetuating a cycle of grief and uncertainty. For many, identifying a suspect like Gary Allan Srery provides only partial relief—knowing the perpetrator does not always bring peace or justice.

The families of Eva Dvorak, Patsy McQueen, Melissa Rehorek, and Barbara MacLean had to wait for more than four decades for the cases to be solved. They might be comforted by knowing the truth, but still, they won't recover their loved ones. Dave Hall, head of the investigation in the 2020s, poignantly noted that despite the search for justice, whether there is a charge or no charge, they aren't fixing anything. For families, it is just an answer.

11
The Hillside Stranglers

It was a cool evening on October 17, 1977, when Yolanda Washington was out in the streets of Los Angeles. She was only 19 years old and was a sex worker. While she was walking by the same places as usual, she was intercepted by two men in police uniforms. She believed it was just another bad night she would have to spend in prison for her illegal activity. Unfortunately, it turned out to be much worse than that.

Yolanda's body was found the next day on a hillside near the Ventura Freeway. She had been brutally assaulted, and the signs of ropes around her neck, ankles, and wrists showed she had been tortured and strangled to death. The killer washed the body to remove any possible evidence, but this didn't prevent the police from knowing she wasn't killed at that place. Later, the police found out that the woman had entered the presumed police car and was killed inside it.

Since the police couldn't gather any evidence, they had no clue about who the killer was. In fact, it would take some time for the police to discover that they weren't after one killer but a team of two. It was only the first of 10 murders in a short period of four months that gripped Los Angeles citizens with fear. All of the victims were women and girls between the ages of 12 and 28, all abducted in the street dressed as police officers.

The crimes were perpetrated by two men who were cousins, Angelo Buono and Kenneth Bianchi. The police then called them the Hillside Stranglers because they dropped their victims' bodies on the hills, and most of them were strangled to death. The conditions of the bodies showed the level of rage and violence unleashed toward the helpless women and girls by the deadly duet.

The family environment in which Kenneth Bianchi and Angelo Buono grew up played a significant role in shaping their paths toward such cruel criminal behavior. Both cousins experienced tumultuous childhoods marked by instability and a lack of nurturing parental figures. Kenneth Bianchi was born to an unwed mother who gave him up for adoption shortly after his birth. His adoptive parents, though providing a more stable environment than his biological parents could have, still struggled with Bianchi's behavioral issues from a young age.

His adoptive mother described him as deceitful and manipulative, qualities that would later manifest in his criminal activities.

Angelo Buono's upbringing was similarly fraught with difficulties. Raised by a single mother after his father abandoned the family, Buono lacked a strong paternal figure and often clashed with his mother. This adverse family dynamic contributed to his early rebelliousness and disdain for authority. Research suggests that children who grow up in unstable or abusive households are more likely to develop antisocial behaviors. Additionally, the lack of positive role models and the presence of negative influences can significantly impact a child's development and future behavior.

Even before they teamed up to become the notorious Hillside Stranglers, both Bianchi and Buono exhibited troubling behaviors that hinted at their potential for future violence. Bianchi's early life was characterized by petty theft, truancy, and lying. He struggled academically and socially, often getting into fights and showing little respect for rules. Bianchi's adoptive mother reported that he was prone to fits of rage and had a disturbing fascination with death. These early warning signs were clear indicators of deeper psychological issues that were never adequately addressed.

Similarly, Angelo Buono displayed a pattern of delinquent behavior from a young age. He dropped out of high school and quickly became involved in a series of criminal activities, including car theft and burglary. Buono's interactions with women were particularly alarming. He exhibited abusive and controlling tendencies in his relationships. This pattern of behavior escalated over time, culminating in acts of extreme violence against women. Studies have shown that early exposure to violence and a lack of intervention can lead to more severe criminal behavior in adulthood.

Growing up in economically disadvantaged neighborhoods, both cousins were exposed to various forms of crime and social unrest. These environments often lacked strong community structures and support systems, making it easier for individuals to engage in criminal activities without fear of repercussion. Furthermore, the transient nature of their communities meant that there was little sense of accountability or lasting connections, allowing them to act with relative impunity.

Bianchi and Buono's relationships within their communities were also telling. Bianchi often moved between different jobs and social circles, never establishing meaningful connections. This transient lifestyle made it difficult for others to notice patterns in his behavior or hold him accountable for his actions. Buono, on the other hand, was somewhat more established in his community but was known for his intimidating and domineering presence. His reputation allowed him to exert control over others, further enabling his criminal activities.

Both Bianchi and Buono associated with individuals who either participated in or turned a blind eye to their criminal activities. This lack of positive peer influence further entrenched their deviant behavior patterns. The absence of consistent parental guidance meant that both boys lacked the moral framework necessary to distinguish right from wrong effectively. In Bianchi's case, despite his adoptive mother's intentions, her inability to provide consistent discipline led to a cycle of escalating bad behavior. Buono's experience was similar. His mother's struggles to manage him allowed him to act without consequence from an early age. Others would later pay the consequences.

The Hillside Stranglers, cousins Bianchi and Buono, wreaked havoc in Los Angeles by employing meticulous techniques and strategies. Their sinister activities left a trail of fear and mystery, captivating the public and law enforcement alike. After Yolanda's murder, they continued their killing rally.

The next victim was even younger, a 15-year-old girl named Judith Miller. She was a runaway and also a sex worker. These girls seemed to be an easy target for the killers who performed as policemen. Judith was standing at a corner when Buono and Bianchi approached. They made her enter the car, and they left. The body was dumped in the residential area La Crescenta. Like Yoanda, Judith was abused and strangled. The Hillside Stranglers already had a method.

Bianchi and Buono's victim selection process was methodical and calculated. They specifically targeted young women who appeared vulnerable, such as those walking alone at night or waiting for buses. By presenting themselves as authority figures, often impersonating police officers, they gained their victims' trust and compliance. This guise allowed them to approach their targets without arousing suspicion, making it easier to abduct them without resistance. They would tell their victims they were going downtown and took them to Angelo Buono's upholstery shop, which served as their hideout.

Once a victim was selected, the execution of the murders followed a disturbingly organized pattern. The cousins used their familiarity with the local area to choose isolated spots for the abductions, ensuring minimal chance of witnesses. They would then coerce the victims into their vehicle, where the true horror began. Physical restraints were employed to subdue the victims, rendering them powerless. The methods of murder were brutal and ruthless, involving strangulation and sexual assault. Each act was carried out with precision, showcasing their chilling resolve and lack of empathy.

Covering their tracks was paramount for Bianchi and Buono. To dispose of evidence and evade capture, they meticulously planned the disposal of the bodies. Victims were often dumped on hillsides or remote locations, hence earning them the moniker "Hillside Stranglers." The choice of these locations was strategic, making it challenging for law enforcement to trace back to the scene of the crime. Additionally, they took great care in removing any physical evidence that could link them to the murders, including wiping down surfaces and disposing of personal items belonging to the victims.

Despite their efforts to remain undetected, the cousins eventually slipped up, leading to their arrest. Sheriff's detective Frank Salerno played a crucial role in piecing together the evidence that exposed their crimes.

The Hillside Stranglers case is a chilling chapter in history of Los Angeles. Law enforcement strategies played a pivotal role in capturing these ruthless killers. Preserving potential evidence was complicated due to environmental factors. However, breakthroughs in forensic science, though primitive compared to modern methods, provided vital clues. One crucial piece of evidence was the seminal fluid found on the victims. While DNA profiling wasn't yet available, other techniques like blood typing and microscopic hair analysis were employed effectively.

The killers had succeeded in evading the cops by removing any sign of evidence. The turning point was when, in May 1978, Bianchi left Los Angeles and went to Washington. He was behind a woman he had fallen in love with and wanted her to marry him. Once in Washington, Bianchi couldn't repress his killing instinct. He kidnapped and killed two teenagers.

Bianchi killed the girls following the same procedure used by the team. Nonetheless, being on his own, Bianchi made a mistake and left evidence at the crime scene and the girls' bodies. This led the police immediately to him the next day.

The crimes in Washington bore striking resemblances to the Hillside Strangler cases. This arrest opened new avenues for the Los Angeles Police Department (LAPD) task force. Faced with overwhelming evidence, Bianchi began cooperating with authorities, leading to Buono's capture. These developments marked a critical turning point in the investigation, demonstrating the importance of persistence and meticulous detective work.

The arrest and trial of Bianchi and Buono were complex and drawn-out processes. Bianchi initially attempted to plead insanity, but his ruse was quickly uncovered. He then agreed to cooperate in exchange for a plea deal, providing detailed accounts of how he and Buono carried out their gruesome acts. This cooperation was instrumental in building a strong case against Buono. The trial garnered massive media attention, and both men were eventually convicted. In 1983, Bianchi received a life sentence at the Washington State Penitentiary, while Buono was sentenced to life imprisonment at a California State Prison, where he died of a heart attack in 2002.

During the investigation, the policemen asked Bianchi about the criminal partnership he had with his cousin. He answered that Buono "was just an easy guy to get with the program".

12

Kent State Shootings— The Tragedy Of May 4, 1970

On the morning of May 4, around 3,000 students and spectators began to gather in the Commons despite the ban on rallies. Some of the students were engaged activists who fought for peace and the common good. One of them was Allison Beth Krause. She had moved to Kent due to her father's job and volunteered at a mental hospital. She was a freshman when she decided to participate in the demonstration as she usually did.

Allison was with two friends, Jeff Miller and Sandy Scheuer. Jeff was a psychology major deeply moved by the fight for human rights and studies about the environment and criminal justice. Allison and Jeff were shot during the protest.

Sandra was a speech therapy major and a member of Alpha Xi Delta sorority. She used to take part in demonstrations, but not that day. She had to attend class, and she was a devoted student. She was shot in the neck when she was walking near the protest toward her class. The same happened to Bill Schroeder, a psychology senior student and member of the Army ROTC. His life was taken with a shot in his chest also when going to class.

How did a peaceful protest comprised mainly of college students end up in bloodshed?

At around 11 a.m., the crowd started growing, and a sense of unease permeated the atmosphere. In response, General Robert Canterbury ordered his men to disperse the protesters. A Kent State police officer announced the order from a military jeep, but the protesters refused to leave. What followed was a tense standoff, with demonstrators shouting and throwing rocks while the Guardsmen equipped themselves with M-1 military rifles and gas masks.

The critical moments that led to the fatal shootings unfolded rapidly. When the protesters ignored the orders to disperse, the Guardsmen fired tear gas into the crowd. The wind conditions made the gas largely ineffective, and the confrontation moved up Blanket Hill and down toward a football practice field enclosed by fencing. Cornered and under a barrage of rocks, the Guardsmen retreated back up the hill. Upon reaching the top, 28 Guardsmen suddenly turned and opened fire on the crowd. Over just 13 seconds, nearly 70 shots were fired. Four students—Jeffrey Miller, Allison Krause, William Schroeder, and Sandra Scheuer—were killed, and nine others were injured. One of the students, William Schroeder, was shot in the back, contrary to some initial reports.

One critical event that spurred the protest at Kent State University was President Nixon's announcement of the U.S. invasion of Cambodia on April 30, 1970. This decision signaled an escalation of the Vietnam War, contradicting Nixon's earlier promises to de-escalate the conflict. The invasion outraged students across the country, leading to widespread protests on college campuses. At Kent State, the announcement ignited a series of demonstrations, reflecting the growing frustration and anger among students.

On May 1, 1970, this anti-war rally took place at Kent State University's Commons area, a common site for various demonstrations. Students gathered to voice their opposition to the Cambodian invasion, delivering fiery speeches against the war. According to eyewitnesses, what started as a peaceful protest quickly turned chaotic when some protesters damaged downtown businesses and set fire to the ROTC building on campus. As a result, the decision was made to call in the Ohio National Guard to restore order. Later that evening, the situation escalated as disturbances broke out in downtown Kent. Protestors clashed with police, resulting in property damage and confrontations. Mayor Leroy Satrom declared a state of emergency and sought assistance from Governor James Rhodes, fearing further violence and disturbances.

In response to the escalating situation, authorities decided to call in the Ohio National Guard troops. On May 2, the National Guard arrived in Kent to maintain order and manage the ongoing protests. Approximately 1,000 Guardsmen arrived on campus, turning the university into a heavily patrolled zone. Despite efforts by university officials to diffuse the situation by banning further rallies, tensions continued to rise. Governor Rhodes made statements condemning the protestors, describing them as "the worst type of people we harbor in America." The militant stance taken by authorities contributed to the tense atmosphere, setting the stage for further confrontation.

On May 3, Guardsmen and students had occasional interactions, but the day remained relatively calm. However, all eyes were on the scheduled protest for noon on May 4. People's attention focused on the demonstration of the following days. The authorities also concentrated all their efforts on a plan to discourage that and any other protest. Nonetheless, nobody expected the tragic outcome.

On May 4, 1970, another rally was planned at Kent State Commons despite a ban on gatherings. As students assembled, the National Guard attempted to disperse the crowd using tear gas. When the tear gas failed to clear the area, Guardsmen advanced with bayonets fixed. The situation rapidly deteriorated, leading to chaos. Amid the confusion, a group of Guardsmen fired into the crowd, resulting in the deaths of four students and injuries to nine others.

The Kent State shootings on May 4, 1970, were a tragic culmination of heightened tensions amidst the Vietnam War era. That day, four students were fatally shot, and nine others were seriously injured. To understand this event thoroughly, it is crucial to delve into the details of how the protest unfolded, the actions of the National Guard, the critical moments that led to the fatal shootings, and the immediate aftermath.

During the Vietnam War era, anti-war sentiment among American students was prevalent and deeply rooted. Many young people felt disillusioned with the government's actions in Vietnam, believing that the war was unjust and unnecessary. This sentiment was pervasive on college campuses, where students organized rallies, sit-ins, and marches to express their opposition. They sought peace and questioned the moral and ethical justifications for the U.S. involvement in Vietnam.

The societal and political climate of the 1960s and '70s significantly fueled student activism. The Civil Rights Movement had already mobilized a generation of young people advocating for social justice and equality. Additionally, the counterculture movement, which promoted alternative lifestyles and anti-establishment values, influenced many students. These movements intersected with anti-war protests, creating a potent mix of activism driven by a desire for change and justice.

The decision to deploy the National Guard and their subsequent actions raised numerous questions about the authorities' handling of the protest. Critics argued that the use of armed troops was an overreaction and exacerbated the tensions. Local law enforcement might have been better suited to handle the situation without resorting to military force. Furthermore, there were debates about whether the Guardsmen were adequately trained for such assignments and if the chain of command properly managed the unfolding events.

The aftermath of the Kent State shootings sparked nationwide outrage and intensified anti-war sentiments. The incident highlighted the deep divisions within American society regarding the Vietnam War and the role of government authority in suppressing dissent. Witnesses and students on campus struggled to comprehend what had just happened. The campus was immediately ordered closed, and it remained shut down for six weeks. The impact of the tragedy on those present was profound. Many witnesses suffered from emotional trauma, and the families of the victims were devastated by their loss. The image of Mary Vecchio kneeling over Jeffrey Miller's body, captured by photographer John Filo, became an iconic representation of the horror of that day. This photograph won a Pulitzer Prize and remains deeply ingrained in the collective memory of the nation.

The Kent State shootings on May 4, 1970, marked a significant and tragic moment in American history. Thousands of students at campuses nationwide protested in solidarity with Kent State, leading to strikes and mass demonstrations. Universities from California to New York saw protests erupt as students voiced their anger against the use of violence on campuses. The tragedy not only intensified the anti-war movement but also highlighted the extent of political and cultural divisions within the United States during the Vietnam War era.

Nationally, the response varied significantly. While some expressed support for the actions of the National Guard, believing they acted in self-defense amid a chaotic situation, while others condemned the use of lethal force against unarmed students. Politicians, civil rights leaders, and activists called for thorough investigations to uncover what had transpired that led to such loss of life.

Numerous legal proceedings and investigations were launched to determine the events of that tragic day. The President's Commission on Campus Unrest, also known as the Scranton Commission, was formed to investigate the incident. The commission's findings concluded that the shootings were "unnecessary, unwarranted, and inexcusable." They recognized that while the protesters had thrown rocks and bottles, the Guardsmen's lives were not in sufficient danger to justify their actions.

Various investigations and court trials ensued, including testimonies from the Guardsmen who maintained that they feared for their lives. However, there was significant disagreement about whether they were truly under sufficient threat to warrant the use of lethal force. In 1979, a civil suit filed by the injured students and the families of the victims resulted in a settlement in which the Ohio National Guard agreed to pay $675,000 to the plaintiffs. As part of the settlement, the Guardsmen issued a statement acknowledging that the tragedy should not have occurred and suggested that alternative measures could have resolved the confrontation.

13

Spring Hill Shooting—The Brisbane Horror

It was another day in Spring Hill, in the suburbs of Brisbane, Australia. It was a quiet community where nothing ever happened. Neighbors knew each other and felt safe. Nobody would say they went out in the streets looking over their shoulders. Nonetheless, September 22, 1976, would be a sad landmark in the town's history.

The streets were crowded with people going to bars and restaurants to have lunch. It was an ordinary day, but it would later be remembered as "violent Wednesday." Donald Galloway was walking near a car park and crossed

Boundary Street at the exact moment a man armed with a .22-calibre rifle and 500 rounds of ammunition opened fire randomly around him. One of the bullets thrown at no special target reached Donald and hurt him. Despite being seriously injured, he survived.

Near him and almost at the same time, 17-year-old Monika Schleuss was also crossing the street toward a shop for brunch. The man with the rifle saw her, and, this time, he pointed his weapon at her head and shot. Monika fell dead on the pavement. Monika's death wasn't enough for the shooter, who continued his uncontrolled fire round.

The shooter was a local cleaner named Robert William Wilson, who had received a diagnosis of schizophrenia. Apparently, he was outraged at being rejected from the model plane club due to his mental health condition. People who knew him later testified and told the police that crafting airplanes was his deepest passion, and being rejected was more than he could take. Somehow, he drove that anger toward the innocent people he found in the street.

After shooting at Donald and killing Monika, Wilson walked down Boundary Street with the rifle on his shoulder. The sidewalks, usually full of children's laughter and friendly conversation, were instead filled with gunshots. The bullets struck windows, fences, and garages, searching for more victims. People ran and screamed, trying to escape from the massacre.

After crossing the street, the gunman opened fire in a general store, and the shooting ended with the death of Marianne Kalatzis, who was 18 years old. She worked in the store owned by her parents. She got shot in her cheek, and although she was taken to the hospital immediately, she died six hours later. Other people were injured, too. Mavis Saunders was standing next to Marianne in the bar and was shot in the chest, though she miraculously lived. Virginia Hollidge, 25, got a bullet in her ankle. Fortunately, it didn't touch any vital areas.

The shooter left the store and entered the barber shop next door. There, he shot again four times and seriously wounded Quinto Alberto. While the shooter was in the barber shop, he heard the sounds of the police approaching. The neighbors had called emergency when they heard the first shots.

The police didn't arrive immediately because they were in the middle of a training session. When the superintendent was informed of what was going on in the suburbs of the city, he gave the order to interrupt the training and headed to Boundary Street. By 1:30 p.m., they were at the crime scene.

The shooter felt cornered, but he didn't end his attack. On the contrary, he moved on and shot a Main Roads engineering draftsman in his back. The man was heading to St. Andrew's Hospital to visit his ill father.

Running away from the police or as part of his killing raid, Wilson walked 1.5 miles and broke into a house where he took hostages to force the police to negotiate with him to surrender. As he walked, he shot again while he sought a place to hide. Finally, he chose Kevin Grove's house. Kevin was trying to reach home to be safe from the shooting, but Wilson pointed the rifle at him and compelled him to let him in. Wilson took five student teachers as hostages and took positions inside the house to wait for the police.

Around 4:00 p.m., the Emergency Squad team arrived at the scene and surrounded the house. Wilson was entrenched inside the house with the five hostages. A police officer could see through the keyhole that the shooter was standing, holding his rifle beside the hostages. About 15 minutes after their arrival, the superintendent authorized the squad to storm the house even though it was risky for the people inside. The shooter could open fire at them at any minute. For almost three hours, there was unbearable tension outside and inside the house. The neighbors remained safe in their own residences but awaited the moment the shooter was captured.

Despite the risk, two officers tore the door down and pointed at Wilson. The strike was so violent that the ladder fell on the hall. They wanted to surprise the shooter to avoid any reaction. Officer O'Gorman aimed to scare the shooter and fired toward him without hitting him, and then fired toward the ceiling. Right after him, officer Krosch fired his weapon toward the floor. For a few seconds, everything was fear and turmoil. Even though no hostage was injured, the plan to scare the shooter failed. He wouldn't drop the rifle or surrender.

It was an instant, but it felt like hours to the hostages who feared for their lives and for the police officers who had to make difficult decisions. The officers took advantage of the confusion driven by their shooting and jumped over Wilson. One of them was able to take the rifle from his hand. With the shooter disarmed, the other officer hit him to overpower him.

Eventually, the two police officers had the situation under control. The shooter was taken to the police station and then driven to prison. By 4:15 p.m. that Wednesday, the horror was over, leaving several victims behind.

The individual behind the Spring Hill shooting had a complex background. Born and raised in Brisbane, Wilson experienced early childhood trauma and exposure to violence, both of which play significant roles in the origins of violent behaviors. His life was marked by numerous personal grievances and crises that compounded over time. He often felt marginalized and misunderstood, setting the stage for his radicalization and subsequent violent actions.

Several key moments influenced his path toward the shooting. Throughout his adolescence, he exhibited troubling behavior and expressed grievances that went unnoticed or unaddressed. In the years leading up to the tragic event, he found validation in past shootings carried out by others, viewing them as inspirational acts rather than abhorrent crimes. This dangerous admiration, coupled with access to firearms, set a deadly course. An increased frequency of legal and illegal procurement of weapons was noted during this period, highlighting another critical factor in the timeline of events.

On the day of the shooting, it became evident that the perpetrator's actions were premeditated. Early in the morning, he gathered his legally purchased and illegally acquired firearms and headed to Spring Hill. The sequence of events unfolded with chilling precision. He first targeted an office building, opening fire indiscriminately, before moving to nearby public spaces. Each location was chosen to maximize harm and instill widespread terror. The shooting spree lasted less than an hour but resulted in the deaths of seven individuals and numerous injuries.

The immediate aftermath of the shooting was chaotic. First responders arrived quickly, but the damage was already extensive. Survivors were rushed to hospitals while local law enforcement began the grim task of securing the area and identifying victims. Families of the victims faced unimaginable grief, struggling to process the sudden loss of their loved ones. For weeks, the community grappled with the emotional and psychological burden of the tragedy.

The aftermath of the Spring Hill shooting in 1976 sent ripples through the Brisbane community, sparking immediate responses that highlighted both the unity and the anguish of the local residents. The incident was an unprecedented horror that shook the town's sense of safety to its core, compelling people to come together in their shared grief and support for one another during this trying time.

Expressions of shock and grief were palpable as news of the tragedy spread. Local residents, struggling to comprehend the brutality of the event, gathered at various locations to mourn the loss of the seven victims. Community vigils became a common sight as people came together to honor those who had been taken from them so abruptly. Churches opened their doors to offer solace and comfort, while local businesses displayed symbols of mourning, such as black ribbons or memorial displays, signifying a collective sadness that pervaded the town. It was not uncommon to see neighbors comforting each other, providing emotional support that was crucial for communal healing.

The Spring Hill shooting in 1976 sent shockwaves across Australia, forcing a national reassessment of gun control laws. In examining the evolution of gun-related violence and crime prevention strategies since the tragedy, it is clear that the Spring Hill shooting served as a pivotal moment. Over time, Australia continued to refine its approach to gun control, culminating in significant actions like the 1996 National Firearms Agreement (NFA) following the Port Arthur massacre. The NFA introduced even more comprehensive reforms, such as the banning of automatic and semi-automatic firearms, mandatory gun buyback programs, and the establishment of uniform firearm licensing standards across states and territories.

Perhaps one of the most telling impacts of these changes is the cultural shift regarding gun ownership and use in Australia. There has been a clear movement toward recognizing firearms not as everyday tools but as potentially dangerous objects that require responsible handling and stringent control.

Wilson was kept in Wolston Park Hospital at Wacol for mental disease patients for three years while he waited for the trial. Four years after the shooting in Brisbane, Wilson was taken on trial. During the trial, the defense exposed the reasons that drove the shooter to that gruesome attack. They attempted to use his mental health condition to plea that he wasn't conscious of his actions. He claimed to have a cloud on his brain that morning and not knowing what he was doing. Moreover, some testimonials said he was friendly and kind, but any of his previous behaviors would give him away as a violent person.

Nonetheless, the jury labeled him as a psychopath and didn't believe the shooter was out of control when he attacked. On the contrary, he shot at people in cold blood. They pleaded Wilson guilty to two charges of murder and four of attempted murder. Wilson will spent the rest of his life in prison.

Please leave a review

If you've made it this far, thank you for joining me on this chilling journey through the darkest corners of crime in the 1970s. I hope these stories left you captivated, intrigued, and perhaps a little shaken, just as they did for me while uncovering them.

As a fan of the true crime genre, you understand how powerful these narratives can be. Now, I need your help to ensure others can discover this book. By leaving a review, you're not only sharing your thoughts and experiences with other readers, but you're also helping fans of true crime find this book.

Thank you for your support and for being part of the true crime community!

Best regards,

Alexander

14

Clifford Cecil Bartholomew— A Family Annihilator

"Hope Forest" doesn't sound like a fitting name for a place of so much bloodshed. A whole family found no hope there. It is a small town about 40 miles south of Adelaide in South Australia. The Bartholomews were a numerous family: the mother, Heather, seven children, and the father, Clifford. He was a 40-year-old truck driver. In 1971, they all lived comfortably in a rented house with seven rooms.

In September, the landscape was beautiful, and the weather was great for the children. Heather's sister-in-law,

Winnis Mary Kean, had come to visit them with her young son, Samuel, who was only two. They came for a couple of days and decided to spend the holidays there. It was a terrible decision.

Early in the morning of September 6, Bartholomew woke up. It was Father's Day in Australia, but instead of making himself breakfast or preparing to have a celebration day, Bartholomew had very different plans.

He took his gun—a .22 caliber rifle—and approached his wife, who was still asleep. He struck her in the head with a mallet and then shot at her with the rifle. The whole house was in silence, and the rest of the family didn't suspect the tragedy that had started in the main room. The killer was walking down the corridor while everybody else was defenseless in their beds.

He slowly walked out of the bedroom he shared with his wife, who was then lying in a poodle of blood. Without making any noise, he went room by room and used the same rifle to shoot at every member of the family. He entered his sons' and daughters' bedrooms and shot them. Neville Kenneth, 19, Christine Heather, 17, Sharon Anne, 15, Helen Joy, 13, Gregory Kym, 10, Roger Clifford, 7, and Sandra June, 4, all were killed with the same rifle.

Some of the children were first hit with the mallet, like their mother. Bartholomew wanted to subdue them and make sure they wouldn't move and he wouldn't miss the shot. Nonetheless, not everything worked for

Bartholomew as he had planned. The children woke up before he reached the bedrooms. Still, that didn't persuade Bartholomew to carry on with his macabre execution.

Two of the children tried to escape from the house. Unfortunately, the runaway path was the same corridor the executioner was walking through. As the children ran, trying to reach the back door, he shot them in the head before they could reach the hall.

Although he killed his immediate family, Bartholomew's job wasn't over. There were others in the house, and that seemed to be their death sentence. Bartholomew headed toward the guest room where Winnis Mary was sleeping with her son, Samuel. He shot Winnis Mary at once while Samuel ran out of the room, probably scared by the noise of the shooting and the blood that came from his young mother. Bartholomew shot him in the back, killing him.

That morning, Bartholomew carried out his horrifying plan with brutal efficiency. He methodically eliminated each family member, ensuring there would be no survivors. The sheer ruthlessness of his actions stunned the community and left investigators grappling to understand the motivations behind such a heinous crime.

Bartholomew's behavior during and after the murders further highlighted his detachment from reality. Eyewitnesses described him as eerily composed, almost indifferent to the horror he had unleashed. This stark contrast between his outward demeanor and the atrocity he committed baffled authorities and fueled speculation about his mental state.

The timeline leading to the gruesome incident began with seemingly innocuous events that gradually escalated in severity. Initially, Bartholomew's outbursts were verbal, consisting of harsh words and threats. As tensions increased, these outbursts became physical, with instances of domestic violence marred by unsettling frequency. Each episode intensified the fear and anxiety within the household, contributing to an atmosphere thick with dread.

The relationships within Bartholomew's family were far from harmonious. Known for his volatile temper, Bartholomew often clashed with his wife and children. The household was reportedly rife with tension, creating an environment where minor disputes could escalate rapidly. Friends and neighbors occasionally witnessed heated arguments, suggesting deep-seated issues within the family dynamic. Not long before the massacre, Bartholomew and his wife had a huge argument in a jealous rage, though the neighbors didn't know the details of what triggered it.

In hindsight, there were warning signs that hinted at the looming tragedy. Bartholomew exhibited behaviors that, if given more attention, might have served as red flags. He became increasingly isolated, withdrawing from social interactions and spending more time alone. His temper flared over trivial matters, causing concern among those who knew him. Additionally, Bartholomew's erratic behavior included unexplained mood swings and fits of rage, which alarmed some but went largely unaddressed.

In the final days before the murder, Bartholomew's behavior became increasingly erratic. He displayed signs of paranoia, convinced that his family was conspiring against him. This belief, whether rooted in reality or a product of his deteriorating mind, drove him to take drastic measures. Despite these clear indicators of instability, no external intervention occurred, underscoring a tragic failure to recognize and address the danger he posed.

Throughout this period, Bartholomew maintained a facade of normalcy in public. Neighbors described him as quiet, if somewhat aloof, never suspecting the horrors unfolding behind closed doors. This duality—presenting a calm exterior while harboring violent impulses—complicated efforts to identify the impending threat.

Clifford Cecil Bartholomew was born and raised in a seemingly typical household. However, digging deeper into his personal history reveals underlying issues that may have contributed to his violent behavior. From an early age, Bartholomew exhibited signs of emotional instability. Those who knew him described Clifford as a withdrawn and solitary individual who struggled to form close relationships. While there is no documented history of severe mental illness, anecdotal reports suggest he may have had undiagnosed psychological issues, possibly stemming from early childhood trauma or neglect.

Several theories attempt to explain why someone like Bartholomew could commit such an atrocious act. One prevalent theory is the concept of "catathymic homicide," characterized by overwhelming anger during an emotionally charged period, leading to a violent release. This theory suggests that Bartholomew experienced a buildup of unresolved tension and emotions, which he eventually catastrophically directed toward his family.

Another theory involves examining Bartholomew's possible perception of control. For individuals with certain personality disorders, losing control over their immediate environment can result in extreme reactions. If Bartholomew felt he was losing control, either within his marriage or financial stability, it might have pushed him toward reclaiming control through violence.

Following the murders, investigators pieced together a timeline that illustrated Bartholomew's calculated approach. His meticulous planning revealed a level of forethought that contradicted any notion of a spontaneous act. By understanding this timeline, a clearer picture of the events and their progression emerged, offering crucial insights into Bartholomew's mindset.

In reviewing the notable interactions and behaviors exhibited by Bartholomew, certain patterns became evident. His increasing isolation was coupled with a fixation on perceived slights and injustices, real or imagined. Bartholomew's inability to manage his anger resulted in frequent confrontations, each more volatile than the last. These interactions served as harbingers of the violence that would eventually engulf his family.

Notably, Bartholomew showed no remorse for his actions in the aftermath. Reports indicated that he remained disturbingly calm during his arrest, showing no signs of guilt or regret. This lack of emotional response puzzled both investigators and psychologists, prompting deeper inquiries into his mental health.

Bartholomew's case also raised important questions about the potential psychological factors at play. His behavior suggested possible underlying conditions that influenced his actions. However, without a comprehensive psychological evaluation prior to the murders, these factors remained speculative. The disconnect between his outward behavior and the gravity of his crime complicated efforts to fully understand his motivations.

Following the horrific family annihilation in Hope Forest, South Australia, the judicial process began with an extensive investigation led by local authorities. The detectives meticulously gathered evidence from the crime scene, interviewed witnesses, and pieced together the events leading up to the tragedy. Their goal was to build a comprehensive case against Bartholomew, ensuring that their findings were robust enough to secure a conviction.

Bartholomew was arrested soon after the crime, facing charges of multiple counts of murder. His arrest marked the beginning of a high-profile court case that captured the nation's attention. During the court proceedings, the prosecution presented overwhelming evidence, including forensic data and testimonies from neighbors who reported hearing disturbances on the night of the incident. The defense attempted to argue mitigating circumstances, citing possible mental health issues, but the stark nature of the crime made it challenging to sway public opinion or the jury's perspective.

The court found Bartholomew guilty, and he received a sentence that reflected the severity of his actions. This outcome underscored the judicial system's firm stance on such heinous crimes, aiming to deliver justice for the innocent lives lost and serve as a deterrent for similar future acts. However, the sentencing did not bring closure to the community or the families affected by the tragedy.

Initially, Bartholomew was sentenced to death, but then it was declined. He was condemned to serve a life sentence, but after eight years, he pleaded for parole, which was conceded by the justice. Eventually, he walked out free and married again. His new wife had seven children, who he helped raise as if he was their father. He had changed his name to Clifford Palmer, and the new family had no idea about the terrible crime he had committed.

They were shocked when they learned about it after Bartholomew's death in 2002.

15
References

Angelo Buono and Kenneth Bianchi. (n.d.). Criminal Minds Wiki. https://criminalminds.fandom.com/wiki/Angelo_Buon o_and_Kenneth_Bianchi

Another victim of serial killer John Wayne Gacy's has been identified using DNA. (2021, October 25). NPR. https://www.npr.org/2021/10/25/1049100466/dna-vict im-serial-killer-john-wayne-gacy

Bardsley, M. (n.d.). *David Berkowitz: The Son of Sam.* Crime Library. https://www.crimelibrary.org/serial_killers/notorious/be rkowitz/20.html

Berry, J. (2023, September 25). *The long shadow: Who were Peter Sutcliffe's victims?.* Radio Times. https://www.radiotimes.com/tv/drama/peter-sutcliffe-vi ctims-long-shadow/

The bone-chilling last words of famous serial killers. (2024, January 30). Times Entertainment. https://timesofindia.indiatimes.com/etimes/trending/the-bone-chilling-last-words-of-famous-serial-killers/photostory/107267451.cms?picid=107267461

Bonn, S. (2024, February 12). *The extreme narcissism of serial killer BTK. Psychology Today.* https://www.psychologytoday.com/us/blog/wicked-deeds/202402/the-extreme-narcissism-of-serial-killer-btk

Campbell, T. (2024, May 19). *Slain Windsor woman among the victims of 1970s serial killer: RCMP.* Windsor Star. https://windsorstar.com/news/local-news/slain-windsor-woman-among-the-victims-of-1970s-serial-killer-rcmp

Chapman, S., Alpers, P, Agho, K, & Jones, M. (2006). 1996 gun law reforms: Faster falls in firearm deaths, firearm suicides, and a decade without mass shootings. *Injury Prevention, 12*(6), p. 365-372. doi.org/10.1136/ip.2006.013714

Charles, M. (2021, September 8). *The capture, escape and recapture of serial killer Ted Bundy.* ThoughtCo. https://www.thoughtco.com/ted-bundy-gets-caught-973179

Carter, K. (2024, May 17). *What we know so far about the serial killer's victims: 'This evil monster has caused so much pain and suffering.'* Calgary Herald. https://calgaryherald.com/news/crime/eva-dvorak-patsy-mcqueen-melissa-rehorek-barbara-maclean-serial-killer-victims

Crime shorts: Unsolved homicide—Claire Gagnon. (2023, October 2). N.B. Crime Stoppers. https://crimenb.ca/2023/10/02/crime-shorts-unsolved-homicide-claire-gagnon/

Claire. (2019, April 30). *Case Notes: S01E07 – The Yorkshire Ripper, part 1 of 5.* En Clair. https://wp.lancs.ac.uk/enclair/2019/04/30/case-notes-s01e07-the-yorkshire-ripper-part-1-of-5/

Claire. (2019, July 31). *Case notes: S01E10 – The Yorkshire Ripper, part 4 of 5.* En Clair. https://wp.lancs.ac.uk/enclair/2019/07/31/case-notes-s01e10-the-yorkshire-ripper-part-4-of-5/

The crucial role of forensic science in upholding social justice. (2024, February 16). *Foster+Freeman.* https://fosterfreeman.com/the-crucial-role-of-forensic-science-in-upholding-social-justice/

David Berkowitz | Son of Sam killer. (n.d.). Crime Museum. https://www.crimemuseum.org/crime-library/serial-killers/david-berkowitz/

Dennis Lynn Rader. (n.d.). Murderpedia. https://murderpedia.org/male.R/r/rader-dennis-otero-family.htm

Dogra, K.K. (2020, July). An investigation into the tragedy of the Peoples Temple in Jonestown. *Kwantlen*

Psychology   Student   Journal,   2. file:///C:/Users/saifs/Downloads/499-Article%20Text% 20with%20identifying%20information%20removed-427 9-1-10-20200731.pdf

Eew18. (2012, May 16). *Hillsidestranglers.* Slideshares. https://es.slideshare.net/slideshow/hillsidestranglers/129 63285

Eigen, J.P. (2012, May 17). *Diagnosing homicidal mania: Forensic psychiatry and the purposeless murder.* Cambridge   University   Press. https://www.cambridge.org/core/journals/medical-histo ry/article/diagnosing-homicidal-mania-forensic-psychiatr y-and-the-purposeless-murder/4E898746D8E21DFB84 4360F8626A4D53

Eldridge, A. (n.d.). Jonestown. In *Encyclopedia Britannica.* Retrieved on July 25, 2024, https://www.britannica.com/event/Jonestown

Ferrarin, E. (2023, February 27). *Who was Timothy 'Tim' McCoy, John Wayne Gacy's first known victim?* A&E. https://www.aetv.com/real-crime/tim-mccoy-victim

Fraser, J. (2010, February 1). *2. Investigating crime.* Oxford University Press EBooks; Oxford University Press. doi.org/10.1093/actrade/9780199558056.003.0002

Guiltenane, C. (2022, February 22). *Hillside Stranglers: Cousins' killing spree terrorizes Los Angeles.* Entertainment D   a   i   l   y   .

https://www.entertainmentdailyuk.com/tv/hillside-stran
gler-who-victims-how-arrested-still-alive/

Hamel, J., Dutton, D. & Lysova, A. (2022, May). Intimate partner homicide and the battered person syndrome. In: *Gender and domestic violence*. Oxford University   Press. https://academic.oup.com/book/43974/chapter-abstract
/369512105?redirectedFrom=fulltext

Hartman, S. (2023, August 10). *This day in history: Infamous serial killer 'Son of Sam' arrested in 1977.* W   C   V   B   . https://www.wcvb.com/article/this-day-in-history-serial-
killer-david-berkowitz-son-of-sam-arrested-1977/408569
78

Hayden, A.V. & Smith, B.H. (2018, August 31). *These are the crime scene photos from the BTK Killer's twisted murders.* Oxygen   True   Crime. https://www.oxygen.com/snapped/crime-time/crime-sce
ne-photos-btk-killer-murders

Hope   Forest   shooting.   (n.d.).   In *Wikipedia.* Retrieved   on   August   5,   2024, https://en.wikipedia.org/wiki/Hope_Forest_shooting

The horrifying murders of notorious serial killer 'Son of Sam.' (2024, July 29). New York Daily News. https://www.nydailynews.com/2023/07/29/the-horrifyi
ng-murders-of-notorious-serial-killer-son-of-sam/

Hughes, G. (2022, January 27). *John Wayne Gacy: Through the papers*. Historic Newspapers. https://www.historic-newspapers.com/blog/john-wayne-gacy-newspaper-analysis/

Innes, M. (2014, June 12). *A signal crimes perspective*. Signal Crimes. doi.org/10.1093/acprof:oso/9780199684465.003.0001

Jenkins, J.P. (n.d.). David Berkowitz. In *Encyclopedia Britannica*. Retrieved on August 6, 2024, https://www.britannica.com/biography/David-Berkowitz

Jenkins, P.J. (n.d.). Ted Bundy. In *Encyclopedia Britannica*. Retrieved on August 6, 2024, https://www.britannica.com/biography/Ted-Bundy

John Wayne Gacy trial: 1980. (n.d.). In *Encyclopedia.com*. Retrieved on August 6, 2024, https://www.encyclopedia.com/law/law-magazines/john-wayne-gacy-trial-1980

Karadjis, S. (2023, July 25). *A haunting school-yard memory: The 1970s schoolboy murders in Sydney, Australia*. Crime Traveller. https://www.crimetraveller.org/2019/05/1970s-schoolboy-murders-in-sydney-australia/

Kent State shooting. (2018, November 2). History. https://www.history.com/topics/vietnam-war/kent-state-shooting

Kettler, S. (2022, December 20). *What was John Wayne Gacy's murder trial like?* A&E. https://www.aetv.com/real-crime/gacys-trial

Lee, W. (2018, December 16). John Wayne Gacy was arrested 40 years ago in a killing spree that claimed 33 victims and shattered the illusion of the safe suburban community. Chicago Tribune. https://graphics.chicagotribune.com/john-wayne-gacy-murders-40-years-later/index.html

Lewis, J. M., & Hensley, T. R. (1998). The May 4 shootings at Kent State University: The Search for historical accuracy. *The Ohio Council for the Social Studies Review, 34*(1), p. 9-21. Kent State University. https://www.kent.edu/may-4-historical-accuracy

Linning, S. (2019, March 28). *The night the Yorkshire Ripper struck for the first time: Heart-stopping moments before survivor dubbed 'Irish Annie' was attacked and left for dead are pieced together in a book that gives the killer's victims a voice.* Mail Online. https://www.dailymail.co.uk/femail/article-6856609/Yorkshire-Ripper-Peter-Sutcliffe-struck-time-Anna-Rogulskyj.html

Lucía. (2021, May 24). Haunted globetrotting: The street with no name and the ghosts of Jubilee Park, Sydney. *The Ghost in my Machine.* https://theghostinmymachine.com/2021/05/24/haunte

d-globetrotting-the-street-with-no-name-and-the-ghosts-of-jubilee-park-sydney/

Luiz, C.D. (2007). *The psychology behind Jonestown: When extreme obedience and conformity collide*. Anna Maria College. https://annamaria.edu/wp-content/uploads/2020/09/Claudia-Daniela-Luiz-Fall-2019.pdf

Mark, O. (2023, May 13). *The Hillside Stranglers, the predators who raped and murdered 10 victims*. ATI. https://allthatsinteresting.com/hillside-strangler

Melton, J. G. (n.d.). Peoples Temple. In *Encyclopedia Britannica*. Retrieved on July 25, 2024, https://www.britannica.com/topic/Peoples-Temple

Morris, C. (2024, May 2). National Guard response to Gaza college protests? Kent State students, faculty say "not so fast." Ideastream Public Media. https://www.ideastream.org/education/2024-05-02/national-guard-response-to-gaza-college-protests-kent-state-students-faculty-say-not-so-fast

1976 Spring Hill shooting. (n.d.). In Wikipedia. Retrieved on August 5, 2024. https://en.wikipedia.org/wiki/1976_Spring_Hill_shooting

O'Brien, D. (2024, February 9). *The Hillside Stranglers summary*. Bookey. https://www.bookey.app/book/the-hillside-stranglers

Picotti, T. & Kettler, S. (2023, August 30). *Inside Ted Bundy's troubled and disturbing childhood*. Biography. https://www.biography.com/crime/ted-bundy-childhood

Picotti, T. & Ott, T. (2023, September 5). *BTK Killer: A timeline of his murders, reappearance, and capture.* Biography. https://www.biography.com/crime/btk-killer-dennis-rader-timeline

Plercy, L. (n.d.). *A&S Psychology researcher unravels serial killer Ted Bundy's mental health*. College of Arts and Science. https://psychology.as.uky.edu/psychology-researcher-unravels-serial-killer-ted-bundys-mental-health

Ramchand, R. & Saunders, J. (2021, April 15). *The effects of the 1996 National Firearms Agreement in Australia on suicide, homicide, and mass shootings.* Gun Policy in America. https://www.rand.org/research/gun-policy/analysis/essays/1996-national-firearms-agreement.html

r/brisbane. (2018). On this day in history: Spring Hill siege 22 September 1976. Reddit. https://www.reddit.com/r/brisbane/comments/9hxlmn/on_this_day_in_history_spring_hill_siege_22/

Remembering the lives of the four slain students. (2020, April 27). Kent State University. https://www.kent.edu/magazine/4slain

Rodriguez, M. (2024, May 18). *Calgary serial-killer flew under the radar in Western Canada for two decades. How did he go undetected?*. Calgary Herlad. https://calgaryherald.com/news/crime/serial-killer

Schorn, D. (2005, September 29). *BTK: Out of the shadows.* CBS News. https://www.cbsnews.com/news/btk-out-of-the-shadows/

Sederstrom, J. (2019, January 31). *Who was Lynda Ann Healy, Ted Bundy's first known victim, and why was the crime scene 'unique?'* Oxygen True Crime. https://www.oxygen.com/martinis-murder/who-was-lynda-ann-healy-ted-bundy-first-known-victim

Smith, T. (2021, June 5). *Surviving Ted Bundy: Women attacked by notorious serial killer share their stories.* CBS News. https://www.cbsnews.com/news/ted-bundy-serial-killer-survivor-stories/

This day in history: Ted Bundy found guilty of killing two sorority sisters. (2024, July 24). KETV. https://www.ketv.com/article/ted-bundy-guilty-sorority-sisters-killing-this-day-in-history/44626309#:~:text=Lisa%20Levy%2C%2020%2C%20(left

Timothy Jack McCoy. (n.d.). Chicago Tribune. https://graphics.chicagotribune.com/john-wayne-gacy-new-victims/blurb.html

The trial: Week one. (n.d.). Execulink.com. https://www.execulink.com/~kbrannen/trial03.htm

Tron, G. (2022, August 3). *'He was an easy guy to get with the program'—Who was 'Hillside Strangler' Angelo Buono?* Oxygen True Crime. https://www.oxygen.com/true-crime-buzz/who-is-angelo-buono-the-hillside-strangers-case

Tron, G. (2021, March 25). *The evidence that helped put "Killer Clown" John Wayne Gacy away for good.* Oxygen True Crime. https://www.oxygen.com/true-crime-buzz/john-wayne-gacy-case-cracked-open-by-key-pieces-of-evidence

Tron, G. (2019, February 14). *If Ted Bundy's trial was today, he may have walked free—Thanks to bite mark evidence.* Oxygen True Crime. https://www.oxygen.com/blogs/how-ted-bundy-got-convicted-is-bite-mark-evidence-credible

Underwood, C. (2016, February 15). *Families of Eva Dvorak and Patsy McQueen still hope for break in cold case.* C B C. https://www.cbc.ca/news/canada/calgary/eva-dvorak-patsy-mcqueen-murder-cold-case-1976-1.3444539

Unsolved cold case: The murder of Claire Gagnon (1970)—Dieppe, NB. (2020, July 18). Canada Unsolved. https://www.canadaunsolved.com/cases/claire-gagnon-unsolved-1970-nb

Unsolved murder—Claire Gagnon (16) in Dieppe, NB Canada found May 25, 1970. (2022, May 26). https://www.websleuths.com/forums/threads/unsolved-murder-claire-gagnon-16-in-dieppe-nb-canada-found-may-25-1970.624953/

Valiente, A. & DelaRosa, M. (2018, September 28). *40 years after the Jonestown massacre: Jim Jones' surviving sons on what they think of their father, the Peoples Temple today.* ABC News. https://abcnews.go.com/US/40-years-jonestown-massacre-jim-jones-surviving-sons/story?id=57997006

Ververis, V., Marguel, S., & Fabian, B. (2019, December 11). *Cross-Country Comparison of Internet Censorship: A Literature Review. Policy & Internet, 12*(4), 450-473. doi.org/10.1002/poi3.228

Wakefield, J. (2024, May 17). *RCMP link Calgary murders to American suspected serial killer who died in prison; believe there are more victims.* Edmonton Journal. https://edmontonjournal.com/news/local-news/rcmp-calgary-serial-killer

Wilhelm, S. (2024, May 20). *Sisters of serial killer victim Eva Dvorak horrified but relieved to fully learn what happened.* Calgary Herald. https://calgaryherald.com/news/sister-of-eva-dvorak-victim-serial-killer-gary-srery

Wilson, D. (2015, February 24). How psychopaths hide in plain sight—a psychological analysis of serial killer

Dennis Rader. Independent. https://www.independent.co.uk/life-style/health-and-families/features/how-psychopaths-hide-in-plain-sight-a-psychological-analysis-of-serial-killer-dennis-rader-10067795.html

Windsor woman killed in 1970s cold case was a 'positive person,' family says. (2024, May 22). CBC. https://www.cbc.ca/news/canada/windsor/windsor-calgary-killer-dna-match-1.7211183

Woodbury, R. (2024, May 19). *N.S. doctor predicted decades ago his daughter's murder would be solved. Now it has been.* CBC. https://www.cbc.ca/news/canada/nova-scotia/seriel-killer-calgary-1970s-nova-scotia-connection-1.7208640

Yang, A., Gowen, G., Taudte, J., Deutsch, G., & Lopez, E. (2019, February 15). *Timeline of many of Ted Bundy's brutal crimes.* ABC News. https://abcnews.go.com/US/timeline-ted-bundys-brutal-crimes/story?id=61077236

Zakaria. (2023, November). *Unraveling the mind of a serial killer: The psychology behind heinous crimes.* Criminal. https://www.vocal.media/criminal/unraveling-the-mind-of-a-serial-killer-the-psychology-behind-heinous-crimes

Zbrog, M. (2020, February 4). *How digital forensics caught the BTK Strangler.* Forensics Colleges.

https://www.forensicscolleges.com/blog/forensics-casefil e-btk-strangler

9 783911 417051